ON THE TIGER'S BACK

by Bernard E. Grady

"ONCE ON THE TIGER'S BACK, YOU CANNOT BE SURE OF PICKING A PLACE TO DISMOUNT."

Undersecretary of State George Ball, 1964 —Discussion with President Johnson on expanding the American presence in the Republic of South Vietnam.

D1714405

BIDDLE
PUBLISHING
COMPANY

PO Box 1305, Brunswick, Maine 04011

Publisher's Cataloging in Publication Data
1-Grady, Bernard E.
2-On the Tiger's Back
3-Vietnam War

Library of Congress Card Catalog Number - 94-070938

ISBN 1-879418-13-4

Cover design by Margaret Biddle and Middy Thomas

This book is printed on recycled paper.

Dedication

This book is dedicated to
the men of the
5th Battalion (Airmobile) 7th Cavalry
who served in the Republic of South Vietnam
during the period August, 1966 to August, 1967,
those who returned
and particularly
those who made the ultimate sacrifice
for their fellow soldiers and for their country.
I believe God caught them even before they fell.

Acknowledgements

The author would like to gratefully acknowledge the assistance of the following individuals. My wife, Christine, and my daughter, Rebecca, for their patience, encouragement and helpful comments through many drafts of this work. COL (Ret.) Trevor W. Swett, Jr. for his comments on the manuscript and his Introduction. LTC (Ret.) Robert Scott, Walter J. Marm, Vivian McCrary Day, Joyce Scott, COL (Ret.) William R. Brown, Professor Walter H. Capps, and Gregory Scott for their comments on the manuscript. LTC (Ret.) Richard L. Belt, Nick Benedetti, COL (Ret.) Victor T. Bullock, Jasper Catanzaro, Roland J. Christy, Esq., Hildegard Swain Frey, COL (Ret.) Martin C. "Duke" Frey, Ron "Red Dog" Gow, Mrs. Dayton L. Hare, Marilyn E. Hitti, CSM (Ret.) Brent L. Hodges, COL (Ret.) Jerry Houston, C.T. Hoy, COL (Ret.) William E. Kail, COL (Ret.) John M. Long, Charles G. Love, David McCabe, Dolly McElroy McKean, CSM (Ret.) Robert Meyers, CSM (Ret.) Jeff Neher, MSG (Ret.) George F. Porod, Orvin R. Raavnaas, Rodney Salvi, Richard W. Smith, CSM (Ret.) Haskel B. Westmoreland, LTC (Ret.) A. J. Wise, and Robert P. Wolicki for their encouragement and assistance in many ways. Julie Zimmerman my editor and publisher for her insight and her assistance in getting the "Tiger" out of the forest and into print.

Table of Contents

An Introduction To The 5th Battalion (Airmobile) 7th Cavalry

by Trevor W. Swett, Jr., Colonel, U.S. Army, Retired

The First Cavalry Division (Airmobile) deployed to Vietnam in mid-1965 with eight maneuver battalions instead of the standard nine. Initially assigned to its 3rd Brigade were the 1st and the 2nd Battalions of the 7th Cavalry, known as the "Garry Owens", a motto passed down from General Custer. Later that year The Cav was authorized another battalion for the Garry Owen Brigade.

At that time all available battalions were already committed for deployment in Southeast Asia or elsewhere in the world. Therefore, the decision was made to find a unit which was just getting organized and would take its soldiers through all the stages of their individual and unit training and train them in the new airmobile concepts. For that reason the 5th Battalion 7th Cavalry was activated at Fort Carson, Colorado in April 1966. Many of its soldiers entered the Army together at Carson and undertook their basic training as members of the 1st Battalion (Mechanized) 11th Infantry. As commander of the 1/11th, I had the privilege of getting to know these fine young citizen soldiers, many of them draftees, practically from the moment they entered the service. I was fortunate to be designated the first commander of the 5/7Cav.

Department of the Army was extremely responsive in providing us with the latest airmobile-related equipment and in assigning one of the Army's finest, Major Victor T. "Tom" Bullock, to fill the all-important Operations Officer slot. Major General Autrey J. Maroun's 5th Infantry Division (Mechanized) filled our officer and noncommissioned officer position vacancies from volunteers throughout Fort Carson. Blessed with these resources, the battalion passed the Continental Army Command's pre-deployment tests with flying colors and, after just four months of extremely intensive training, deployed by sea to Vietnam, arriving in early August.

By that time most of the battle-hardened veterans of The Cav had completed their one year tour and were returning home. The challenge given to me personally by the division commander, Major General John Norton, was that the 5/7Cav would be the link between the Division's departing "first edition" of experienced air cav troopers and their replacements, the "second edition", soon to arrive by the thousands. We would provide the continuity in tactics, techniques, esprit-de-corps and victories in battle.

In late October, after viewing the decisive results of our third major engagement with the enemy, General Norton said to me, "In the history of the U.S. Army, I am sure that no battalion has ever made a finer entry into battle than the 5th Battalion 7th Cavalry."

Those are words I shall never forget. General Norton's challenge had been met and the 5/7Cav fought on with distinction throughout the Vietnam War—a distinction which included the award of the Congressional Medal of Honor to Lewis Albanese, William D. Port and Hector Santiago-Colon.

On the Tiger's Back is the story of the original 5/7Cav "grunts"—their ups, their downs, their pride in their accomplishments, their horror as they experienced the tragedy and the anguish of war and its effect on friend and foe, soldier and civilian. This is also about leadership—of sergeants, lieutenants and captains, and those who commanded this extraordinary battalion. The book is a collage of unforgettable experiences and deep reflection, from the frightening baptism of fire to the long awaited rotation back to the U.S.A.

Out of respect for their privacy, the names of certain

individuals are fictitious. Nevertheless, these accounts of events which occurred during the first year in combat of the 5th Battalion 7th Cavalry are true. From them you will sample the personality and flavor of this unique battalion made up of unsung heroes who sacrificed greatly for their country.

Garry Owen!

Bethesda, Maryland
December, 1993

Author's Note: There is no doubt that the success achieved by any Army officer is dependent in large measure on the quality of men he commands. Perhaps the high caliber of the men who served in the 5th Battalion 7th Cavalry is suggested by the fact that, of the twelve lieutenant colonels assigned to command the battalion during the Vietnam War, four became generals—one 4-star (John A. Wickham became Army Chief of Staff), two 3-stars and a brigadier. In addition, Larry Budge, first commander of Charlie Company, achieved the rank of major general.

Colonel Trevor Swett, our first battalion commander, was personally presented The Silver Star Medal for gallantry in action while commanding the 5/7Cav, by the President of the United States. Colonel Swett accepted the award on behalf of his men. I have never, before or since, been privileged to be acquainted with or work for a finer gentleman.

Preface

The Vietnam War was a tragedy set in a land of extraordinary beauty. The country's magnificence was best appreciated from the sky—unremittingly blue, frequently interrupted by great, cumulus whites—where one looked down onto a lush, green patchwork of rice plants growing in watery paddies. Chalk-white beaches separated the indigo South China Sea from the land, a line of sand broken by the outpouring of rivers meandering from the mysterious, forested mountains which dominated the western landscape.

A quiet beauty characterized the people of that gentle society—hard working planter-gatherers or fishermen, whose pretty almond-toned children were quick to laugh, if only with magnificent dark eyes—a community which flowed with nature and its seasons. In the larger towns lithe women in provocative ao dais and old men who resembled Confucius lived amid ancient temples and colorful store fronts in a land steeped in tradition.

Up close, however, amid the graceful palm trees and in the deep grasses, were rusting barbed wire, death dealing land mines, gene altering defoliants and the refuse of war both material and human. The heavens had become a highway for a shell; people fell to unseen bullets and to booby traps.

Vietnam has been described as both an electronic marvel and a communications stench—a nightly portion of blood and burning huts with your mashed potatoes and gravy. This blitzkrieg of sound bites competing for air time created for many at home what the war must have been, and thereby doomed a generation of America's best to undeserved scorn.

Somewhere between the beauty and the stench is the real story of Vietnam. How best to tell that story? How best to describe the evils and the crimes that are a part of war, the demoniac passions, the horrors and the carnage of battle, the fear, as well as the selfless heroism?

Perhaps the participants, both soldier and civilian, can show us Vietnam, and thereby show us war itself. Perhaps it is best to understand what befell those most affected, those whose stories are recounted herein, those who rode the back of the Vietnamese tiger.

Chapter 1

A Passage of Lines

Staff Sergeant Will Fowling must have been very uneasy. The hillside was a bitch—steep and slippery in the wet. Soaked from the rain that coated the brush, he was trying to carefully work his way through, back up the slope, without announcing to every VC in Binh Dinh Province where he was. The mist had abruptly turned everything black in front of him. He could distinguish the crest of the hill from the lighter horizon to the west, but he was on the eastern side and couldn't see objects much more than six feet distant.

The battalion commander had decided to set up the listening post forward of the artillery battery. A good decision. Visibility down that rotten hill, even in daylight, wasn't very good because of the dense, high brush. The perimeter definitely needed some early warning in the event the VC massed for an attack, and Colonel Swett wasn't too confident in the fighting skills of the artillerymen on the perimeter. They were splendid with their cannons, but no one knew how good they would be with a rifle when the chips were down. Best to get someone out in front of them.

Will Fowling had drawn the job of setting up the listening post. Ordinarily, the task would have fallen to the infantry company manning the perimeter. Some grunt sergeant should have hustled his boys down there, but because the artillerymen were holding that portion of the defenses, the Old Man had asked Captain Jerry Houston, the Headquarters Company Commander, to have one of his sergeants position a fire team out front.

Later, when he was coherent, the Artilleryman would say that he had gone beyond ordinary fear, beyond the worst nightmare, beyond what we think of as terror, to a point where his body refused to respond as he wished. At that point a great chill slowly coursed through his muscles, causing some of them to lock up, some of them to shake uncontrollably, and one of them to relax involuntarily, releasing the warm liquid that ran down his leg and soaked his pants and brought him back to reality.

5/7Cav commanding officer Trevor W. Swett, Jr. (right) with Captain Jerry B. Houston, Headquarters Company Commander

The bout of terror wasn't supposed to happen, not to him. Artillery was his branch, not Infantry. His job was with the big guns just behind, not in a damn foxhole looking into the black void to his front, straining for all he was worth to catch again the noise he was certain he'd heard out there.

Just minutes prior he could see the scrub trees and man-high grasses that covered the flank of the hill on which his gun battery was located. Now, the misty rain and low clouds off the South China Sea had hastened the retreat of twilight, blotting out the detail of the landscape, enveloping his visual sense in a fuzzy blackness. However, above the sounds of the rain, the Artilleryman's sharpened hearing seemed to compensate for his loss of vision, and in that ink to his front, he could discern the noise he'd noticed earlier, growing louder, coming nearer. He was certain that something, or someone, was moving up the hill toward his position.

He turned hurriedly, panic threatening to overcome him, wanting to be sick, and looked back toward the tubes, hoping fruitlessly to find some help. The upper portion of the gun muzzles with their flash suppressors were all he could discern, indistinctly, against the horizon. There were supposed to be two more warm bodies in this hole with him. Hours ago his sergeant promised him two more goddamned sets of eyes and ears, but none had come yet. Son of a bitch probably forgot. There was the temptation to run back to the gun emplacement, find the sarge and have him come down to this wet, muddy, uncomfortable hole and listen for the sound; but the Artilleryman had learned the rules and he knew you didn't ever leave your guard post until properly relieved—never, never, ever. A person could be shot for that, he thought, and the idea nearly caused him to laugh aloud. At that point the Artilleryman wasn't sure what would be worse, this hole and the terrifying noise, or a swift shot in the head. But his mirth quickly faded and he checked behind him again; still no help.

Infantrymen were accustomed to this shit, he reasoned. They were familiar with pulling guard, dealing with noises in the night, but the damn rifle company assigned the task couldn't cover the entire perimeter enclosing his battery and the infantry battalion headquarters situated with it. Therefore, artillerymen were filling in a fifty meter gap in front of the tubes. No question, gunners like himself shouldn't be here, but there was no help for him now. The thing was just to his front, at a spot where the hill started to level off, coming directly at him.

He was new to this terror, new in-country, and not one of those mountain men types who could shoot your buttons off at three hundred meters. He grabbed another quick look behind him without a satisfactory result. He had no choice now. And the Artilleryman—his entire body trembling from the rush of adrenalin, sweating profusely despite the chill of the wet night, the veins in his temple and in his neck pulsating violently with each wild heart beat, certain the audible pounding its pumping produced in his ears could surely be heard by whatever was threatening him—snapped the safety off his rifle with a click that was much too loud for comfort, and aimed at what appeared to be a crouched black form now carefully stepping over some cut brush.

Staff Sergeant Fowling knew his standard operating procedures pertaining to going through defensive positions, "a passage of lines"—one of the most dangerous military maneuvers. Accompanied by the men who would compose the listening post, he had carefully checked out through one of the artillery positions, telling the artillerymen he would return shortly. No problem; he knew the artillery had been alerted he was going out and back. However, Will Fowling was able to see then—still twilight. When he returned, all light was gone and he no doubt wondered if he was lost. However, with a little luck, that same position was the one just coming into view through the gloom to his front, an area where the earth had been dug up to construct a fighting position and had been thrown forward down the hill, creating a patch of ground distinctly lighter in color than the surrounding area. Good infantrymen would have camouflaged that earth. Gave the position away. That had to be the position through which he'd checked, or was it?

Will Fowling was almost there. He stepped over some cut brush and froze as he heard a metallic click. He saw an indistinct flash of light and, with a ringing in his ears, was instantaneously and violently propelled backward down the hill by a sharp pressure in his midsection.

Captain Duke Frey, in his capacity as our air liaison officer (S-3/Air), was the guy charged with all liaison between the battalion and the various aircraft units supporting our combat operations. He constantly wrestled with the problems of getting the troops to the birds and the birds where we wanted them when they were needed. That day Duke had managed to get all his missions run and all the companies in place before the weather turned foul and the choppers were grounded. Time to relax. Normally, nothing in combat went as planned, always a glitch somewhere, particularly since we were so new to combat; but not that day. With everyone in place, the battalion could continue operations in the morning despite the weather.

Duke was located with the support units at Landing Zone Hammond near Phu Cat, at that time the hub of Cav activities on the central coastal plain south of Bong Son. Night had just fallen when the battalion radio net, quiet to that point except for the routine sitreps, came to life with the voice of Major Bullock, the battalion operations officer (S-3), calling for a medevac. Duke was struck by the fact that his boss, himself, was making a call which would normally be transmitted by an enlisted radio/telephone operator; additionally, there was a very detectable air of urgency in the major's normally controlled voice.

Duke called the medevac people. His effort produced the nonresult he expected. Their duty officer said "no way". Conditions were far below flying minimums, particularly for a night flight. Duke returned to the net, giving Major Bullock a negative on the medevac.

Few mortals ever saw Tom Bullock take no for an answer if he thought there was any conceivable way to get the job done. Therefore, I was not surprised to hear the S-3, in his best don't-give-me-that-bullshit voice, demand that his subordinate get a medical evacuation chopper. Duke had at the task again, this time speaking directly to the commander of the chopper company, with no luck. He even called to the Cav main base at An Khe, only to get the same negative result. With zero visibility weather, even a pilot's commanding officer couldn't order a flight. Someone would have to volunteer to fly the mission, but volunteers were scarce that night and no one could blame them.

At the Bravo Company headquarters on another hill just north of the battalion HQ, I listened to the drama unfolding on the radio net while trying to write a letter home to Christine, my wife. I knew instinctively that someone must be in deep trouble for the operations officer to be calling for the medevac in those conditions. That feeling was reinforced when, after Duke twice gave a negative, none other than the battalion commander himself came on the radio and, disregarding radio discipline, transmitted in the clear: "Unless we get a medevac here soon, we're going to lose a damn fine November Charlie Oscar." The Colonel had one of his best NCOs down, and the man wasn't going to be around long.

Duke Frey was universally regarded as an extremely competent officer, but competence and a quarter wouldn't get you a cup of coffee that night, or so I thought. Conditions were simply awful. What was needed was a salesman and after that a hero, and if anyone could sell a pilot on flying that night, Duke was the guy. He performed that miracle, and about ten minutes later announced a dustoff was on its way from the evacuation hospital in Quin Nhon, about thirty-five kilometers south. A noticeably relieved Major Bullock acknowledged the success.

I ducked out from under the makeshift poncho tent which served as our company HQ, and squinted into the

CPT Duke Frey, S-3 Air, coordinates wtih company commander on the airfield at Kontum.

night toward the battalion LZ which was less than five hundred meters away. There was nothing to be seen. A fine mist and thick clouds made even the horizon nearly indistinguishable. Being a city boy, I never ceased to be amazed at how complete the blackness was in a land where there are no street lamps and lights from urban areas to artificially brighten the horizon. The darkness was so intense I couldn't see my gear sitting on a large pile of C-ration cases, which I knew were just a few meters away. Yet, I marveled, some chopper pilot was about to fly into that murky void and risk his life, that of his copilot and crew, and half a million dollars in equipment to save a man he didn't know. I didn't pray much in Vietnam, but standing there with the mist soaking my hair, I put in a word with the Man upstairs for the injured NCO and for the medevac crew.

Straight line navigation from Qui Nhon to that LZ, a pinpoint in the blackness, was virtually impossible. There was just one way to fly that extremely dangerous mission under those conditions. The pilot activated the powerful spotlight in the underbelly of the HU-1B, aimed the beam at National Highway 1, and flew that road at tree top level straight up the coastal plain. Fortunately, the battalion LZ was within sight of the highway. When the chopper's engine was audible at the landing zone, the S-3 had him turn on all his lights, and was able to talk him into the pickup point which the Old Man had ordered to be lighted with every available flashlight they could muster, security and the VC be damned.

From my vantage point, I could just make out the illuminated LZ, an indistinct mass of fuzzy brightness off in the mist, and finally I could hear and see the chopper arrive, a noisy spot of light descending out of the black. As the bird departed we could hear Lieutenant Colonel Swett come on the radio to the pilot and thank him with a sincerity I could almost feel. The pilot nonchalantly responded, "No problem, any time," but we all knew the guy was sweating marbles. Shortly, he was gone into the night, the belly light fading rapidly amid the whop-whop-whop of the rotor blades as the bird moved off.

The lights on the LZ were extinguished and the radios returned to their voiceless hissing. Later, Duke Frey broke radio silence with the terse message that the November Charlie Oscar was dead on arrival at Qui Nhon.

I ducked back into the poncho tent to finish my letter.

"*. . .Well, Hon, I'll close now and get some shut eye. Nothing much happening here except for all this rain and flooded rice paddies. I have three pair of socks with me. All of them are soaking wet or damp, and loaded with sand from the bottom of the paddies. I ordered up fresh ones for all the men. They'll come on the a.m. supply chopper. Take care. Don't worry. Haven't seen any bad guys yet. Miss and love you.*

Bernie."

SSG William O. Fowling, on 18 October 1966, atop a hill the Old Man had inadvertently but appropriately named LZ Bloodstone, as a consequence of friendly fire, became the first noncommissioned officer in our battalion to spill his blood and die in Vietnam. I was filled then with a vague feeling of irony at that death, incongruous as it was in contrast to what I had been conditioned to think war would be. Clearly, for the 5th Battalion 7th Cavalry, this aspect of our entry in the war lacked any semblance to the onset of a new heroic age for our storied Garry Owen regiment. Death was the only constant.

Chapter 2

Enemy At The Well

We entered the hamlet by wading through a scum covered, shallow lake, up to our knees in muck. That was the safer way. The smart money didn't saunter through the main gate. The village was typical, except perhaps smaller than most—no more that a dozen fawn-colored huts. It was bounded on one side by that stagnant lake, and on the other by acres of ripening rice, a lush green blanket, broken here and there by bare paddy dikes, a study in greens and browns. The dwellings were unremarkable for that area—steeply-pitched thatched roofs, mud-over-reed sides, a few pane-less windows, entrances without doors, dirt floors. They were clustered irregularly around the village well, a hand-dug affair about five feet in diameter, encircled by a raised platform of dried clay. The raised area was rounded at its edge and smooth, worn so by countless bare feet come to fetch the water. The wall of the well was six inches wide and elevated from the platform about three feet, to prevent children from toppling in, no doubt. A very typical Vietnamese well.

Where I came from a well was constructed of stone or brick and mortar, rather than the hardened clay. My well looked like a quaint wishing well, covered with a sloping roof to prevent the Fall leaves from cascading in and foul-ing the bottom. This one had no cover; the coconut palms shading the village apparently didn't pose that problem. The well in my front yard had a hand crank to hoist up the water bucket; the Vietnamese version just had a long, thick rope which dangled into the water below. Esthetically, this was a rather sterile well, not at all picturesque.

Of course, the significant difference between the wells was that this one was alive, utilized, whereas the hole in the ground at home was simply a quaint relic of the past. To this small Vietnamese village, their well was the center of social life, where the women came together during their daily chores to exchange gossip or the news of the day from distant hamlets. But most critically, it was the source for the fluid necessary for life itself.

For such a tiny village to have a well was atypical. I had been in-country long enough to realize many rural Viet-namese were forced to obtain their water from streams and

Typical village well with women drawing water

ponds which were fouled at times by farm animals or by humans. I had observed the mamma sans walking long distances to a larger village where a well was located, laden with heavy crocks or tins slung from carrying sticks. This was a fortunate village, indeed. I could see little evidence of any really good water about, save this well.

We were out winning the hearts and minds of the people that day, out chasing Viet Cong in order to destroy them and give these poor folk some peace of mind, some freedom from tyranny. That was the gospel according to General Westmoreland. But the enemy was nowhere to be found that forenoon, at least not as yet.

The day was hot and humid. In no other place have I experienced air as hot and as heavy with moisture. The footfalls of Bravo Company created a faint, knee high dust cloud as we moved through the hamlet. As usual, the houses were empty, the occupants having fled the armed, green-clad giants whose intentions they could not fathom, and whom they feared. Empty except for one ancient, squatting on his haunches in front of a hut, shaded by the overhanging thatch. He was attired in calico noir, short pants revealing two brown, sinewy sticks for legs, with bare feet. Wrapped around his knees were two equally emaciated arms extending from his short sleeved, loose fitting shirt. A conical, straw hat thrust back on his head was held in place with two black ribbons bowed together beneath his chin. His face was colored burnt mahogany, wrinkled, clamp-jawed, with a wispy goatee and droopy mustache stained yellow. His dark eyes were intent, but his expression impassive, almost weary. The only life about him was the occasional movement of those chin whiskers, blown by a gust of hot air.

Wells were of interest to me. I was intrigued with the manuals on counterinsurgency which depicted the Viet Cong's underground tunnel systems. Sometimes the tunnels had an entrance in the sides of a well, hidden beneath the water line.

Curious, I peered into the depths. My face on that hot day was met with a cool, musty dampness rising from the liquid surface about twenty feet below. The water was undisturbed and mirrored blue sky and puffy white clouds. The serene picture was broken only by the silhouette of my helmeted head and indistinct features.

I couldn't perceive what was beneath the water's surface. The rope disappeared into the depths. There was no tension on it as I pulled it up and no bucket on the end to haul out the water. I thought that unusual at the time, not realizing these poor people couldn't afford a communal bucket and probably attached their own vessels to draw up their needs. That rope appeared to be much heavier than necessary for drawing water. Perhaps, I thought, with the training manuals still in mind, it was actually used to lower the VC into some hidden grotto beneath the surface. Peering in again, I continued to see no sign of life below which would indicate the presence of an enemy, nothing but my darkened face, the blue sky now turned grey by a black cloud passing overhead.

We civilized peoples don't think much about wells. We depend on faucets. They are important; they equate to water; they represent progress. Civilized people with faucets and pipes don't think much about the cool, unadulterated liquid at the bottom of a well. I didn't think about it that day, even though my canteens contained a substance tasting much like the effluent from a chemical plant, the result of "purification", making the stuff fit for human consumption. So, I simply dropped a hand grenade into the well and ducked back from the opening.

The weapon hit the surface with a plop and exploded seconds later in the depths with a hollow, muffled, thud-like sound. I looked in. The surface was now broken with pieces of blackened sticks and debris. There were no bodies floating on the surface, no blood in the water; there was just water, now very, very muddy.

The old man came to life and shuffled, bent-backed, to replace me at the well's rim as I walked away. He looked in and started an excited jabbering, angrily gesturing at me in a threatening manner.

I didn't comprehend his anger just then, didn't realize I had been successful only in blowing out the bottom and sides of the well. For some time to come, perhaps forever if the concussion had closed off the water source, the well would be unusable. When the villagers returned, the old man would explain how the American had ruined their well, fouled their water, greatly complicated their lives.

That understanding would come to me only much later, too late. I was continuing on my way to win hearts and minds, and there were other villages and other wells to check out. In time, I would realize that I had found the enemy that noon. The enemy was ignorance. The enemy was me.

Chapter 3

How's It Going, Top?

First Sergeant Dayton L. Hare, Jr. was a military policeman in the Second World War, an artilleryman in the Korean Conflict, and now he was an infantryman on his way to Vietnam. He announced those facts to me one day with a noticeable smile of self-satisfaction.

I'm reasonably certain your average infantry types didn't give much thought to being a grunt. Being infantry was simply something which happened when you didn't have much in the way of technical skills, such as engineering or medicine, to give you a leg up. First Sergeant Hare was different, however. He wanted his C.I.B.

"Missed getting it in WW Two and Korea," he explained. "Not that I didn't do any fighting. There was plenty of that. Just didn't have the right MOS. But I'll get it this time."

The first sergeant was speaking of the Combat Infantryman's Badge, an award given only to an infantryman who has served with an infantry unit in a combat zone. Because he had a military police and an artillery military occupational specialty (MOS), he was denied the badge in his two earlier combat experiences.

Our talk wandered over many topics, including why he hadn't retired and avoided pulling a combat tour. The C.I.B. was his answer. Additionally, he wasn't quite ready to leave the Army for the small ranch where he resided with his wife, son and two young daughters. I didn't broach what was a very sensitive topic with him, but I was certain Sergeant Hare could have gotten out of the combat tour without leaving the Army. He had a hearing loss from hanging around those artillery cannons. Had he chosen to press the matter, the Top could have honorably served in a nice, soft slot in the States or any other noncombat position he wanted, and never set foot in the Republic of South Vietnam. However, Dayton Hare wasn't the type to avoid a tough assignment.

I hesitate to describe anyone as a patriot or a hero—he was both in reality—but the Top was more properly described as a man, not the macho type, but a guy who saw a job to be done and, tough as the task might be, he was going to do it. He had chosen to be a soldier. That is what he did all his life, and he was a good one. Just because he was now near the end of his career was no excuse to duck out on one last war. Forget all that stuff about wanting his C.I.B. That was just a cover for something much more fundamental and splendid. Sergeant Hare knew that he had some very valuable qualities to offer—experience, maturity, common sense. I had the clear impression he felt an obligation to impart some of that good stuff on us youngsters who were to fight our first war. He had one other important trait necessary to do a good job—courage.

Many years after the war I had occasion to correspond with the Top's wife. She told me of his frame of mind prior to our departure:

"He was a true soldier. He came home and spoke of those young boys often and I was just waiting for him to tell me he was going also. He could not watch the battalion get on that plane and stay here."

For my part, I came to feel absolutely blessed when the gods assigned me to Bravo Company. By virtue of a stay in graduate school after commissioning, I was a very senior, but woefully inexperienced, first lieutenant (soon to be a captain) who found himself the executive officer of a combat-bound, airmobile rifle company, without ever having set foot in a company area. Fortunately, I recalled the advice of one of my more knowledgeable ROTC instructors who recommended that we should, in all situations, "latch onto the First Soldier and do what he says." You better believe I did just that.

In that regard, the Top and I developed a shared system of communication which I used whenever I was in need of military advice. Instead of wounding my pride by coming right out and asking for help with a problem for which every other self-respecting lieutenant would already have the answer, I would inquire, "How's it going, Top?"

He had the ability to fathom that the question was more a cry for help than an inquiry concerning his health, and would reply, "What can I do for you, Sir?"

1st Sergeant Dayton L. Hare, September 1966

I'd ask my questions; he'd give answers. Our system worked very nicely. The answers were invariably correct.

Dayton Hare looked to be the prototypical Army First Sergeant. He was tough (at least on the exterior), lean and wiry, short of stature, but imposing of presence. He had reddish blond hair with a not too severe crew cut and penetrating blue eyes that could bore completely through you. His trademark was an ever-present stump of a cigar clamped between his lips, which seem always to be unlit. The sergeant was forever taking the thing carefully from his mouth with thumb and forefinger, and looking at it with a frown, as if the poor cigar was a raw recruit who had committed some unpardonable offense. He would then commence the relighting ritual, using great numbers of matches, trying without much success to draw air through the soggy end mashed flat by his unconscious chewing. After a time the cigar would refuse to relight no matter how diligent the effort, a new one would be produced from a never exhausted supply in his desk, and the process would begin anew.

The Top went all the way to Vietnam with a cigar in his mouth, much to the consternation of the crew of the ship which carried the bulk of the battalion there. Of course, smoking wasn't permitted just anywhere, particularly since there was ammunition aboard; but the Top never lit the cigar, he just clamped the thing in his jaws the entire trip and chewed on its end. Invariably, some junior seamen would march up to the Top and order him, with great authority, to get rid of the cigar. The Top's eyes would narrow as he transfixed the guy with one of his most potent stares, and he would inform the poor fellow that he'd think, (the emphasis clearly was on the thinking), about getting rid of his cigar, "but don't count on it, sonny."

The old French airfield just North of An Khe City had been appropriated by the 1st Cav and was utilized as the primary, fixed-wing landing field for the division. The facility was appended to the eastern edge of the defensive perimeter and was nearly surrounded with rice paddies. The battalion flew there from the port of Quin Nhon. As soon as we landed at An Khe, Sergeant Hare marched down the ramp of the aircraft and immediately applied a match to a fresh cigar. The smell of the stogie was a relief from the assaults of aviation fuel.

No sooner had the tobacco odor started to waft about than the Top took a deep breath and announced, "Smells just like Korea."

After that statement he hesitated for a few moments, surveyed the rice paddies around us, and then, in his best pedagogical manner and tone, said, "You know they fertilize the fields over there with the stuff from the bottom of the latrine." He had a serious look on his face. Another deep breath confirmed the first observation. "Yes Sir, just like Korea."

I couldn't smell a thing but the cigar.

Vietnam wasn't Korea, but I guess Army paperwork hadn't changed much in the interim, because Top came into his own when the time arrived for getting the company HQ squared away for combat. He was even better at getting things done in the field. I watched him carefully and, like thousands of greenhorn officers before me, learned everything from my first sergeant. He was no desk bound first soldier, and no slacker humping the bush. Once, he contracted a painful ear infection, but went to the battalion aid station only to get some medication and returned immediately to the field. The Top would never want the troops to see him at sick call.

The one other thing First Sergeant Hare wanted from Vietnam besides his C.I.B. was a set of Noritake Ivory China from Japan. His wife very much wanted a first class set of dinner china and the Top was going to surprise her by having one shipped home. Noritake was well known for its quality and beauty, but wasn't carried in the stateside post exchanges; the expense of Noritake in an off-post store was a luxury few military people could manage to squeeze into their budgets. I wasn't surprised, shortly after we arrived, to discover the Sergeant had already rounded up a

PACEX catalog. (PACEX was an acronym for Pacific Exchange, the high quality but low price Sears-Roebuck equivalent for military personnel stationed in the Far East.) Top came into our orderly room tent with a face that was one complete smile, pulled up a seat next to me and commenced showing pictures of every Noritake place setting available. There were quite a few well thumbed pages of them, and in the center of one, he had circled a particular pattern.

"That's the one," he said with little-disguised excitement, poking a finger at the circled setting. "You like it?"

He said that without expecting an answer, and I hardly got my "beautiful" out before he followed quickly with, "That's the one the wife will like. Couple of paydays and I'll have saved enough," he said, carefully placing the catalog in his field desk.

The first day of the month was payday, even in the Vietnam bush. Combat troops had prearranged for the vast bulk of their money to go home to their wives or to a bank, but they received a few dollars in cash to spend when they could get to the Brigade PX. As the company Executive Officer, it was my duty to disperse the funds. That was my task on November 1, 1966, and I had returned to Ah Khe by late afternoon, after completing the job. Having returned the paperwork to the Division Paymaster, I checked into the personnel shop.

The day was all but gone by then, and a heavy rain fell through a foreboding twilight. As I entered, the S-1, Captain Bill Brown, had a concerned look on his face. He explained that Company B had engaged a very sizable Viet Cong unit. The battle was still winding down. Bravo Company had prevailed in that the VC had broken contact. Unfortunately, however, there were friendly casualties.

As Bill filled me in on what he knew, Rod Salvi, Bravo's company clerk who was on the phone getting the casualty reports from the forward area, literally screamed, "Oh my God, the bastards killed the First Sergeant!"

That morning two platoons from the 1st Squadron 9th Cavalry had been sent out to recon the area near the sizable village of Hoai Nhon, a suspected base for a large enemy force. Almost immediately, both were in contact with what turned out to be an entire battalion of Viet Cong. (Captured documents later identified the enemy as the 93rd Battalion of the 2nd Viet Cong Regiment.)

Both 1/9 Cav elements were quickly pinned down and called for reinforcements. First Platoon of our own Alpha Company was the only friendly unit in the immediate vicinity, but as it approached the village, very concentrated automatic weapons immobilized it. The brigade commander then called for Captain John Hitti's Bravo Company, apparently still not realizing he was facing an enemy battalion. By late afternoon, John completed his airlift into an LZ hurriedly named Susan, and assumed command of all forces on the ground. He put Second Platoon, commanded by 1LT William Kail, on line with Third Platoon, com-

CPT John Hitti (left) and LT Bill Kail

manded by 1LT Ralph Cryer, and attacked. First Platoon and the Mortars were in reserve, but by the time the engagement was finished, everyone saw heavy action.

The attack had to be made across open stretches of rice paddies. There were snipers in the trees, and the VC had a variety of heavy weapons. The 93rd withdrew after dark, uncharacteristically leaving forty-three of their own dead on the battlefield along with many of their weapons, attesting to the fact that they were soundly beaten and trying to exfiltrate at all costs. Third Platoon took the worst beating on our side, with six killed and one wounded. Bill Kail had two go to Graves Registration and three to the hospital. The headquarters element lost a single soldier, Dayton Hare.

When I commanded Charlie Company and my first sergeant, Haskel B. Westmoreland, was wounded and hospitalized, I learned that losing the first soldier is akin to having your father die. In combat, the company commander depends on the guy like his right and left hands. Suddenly cut down, it's a particularly difficult loss.

Next day I rejoined the company at the same LZ where they were inserted the previous day. John Hitti, a tough, professional soldier who had seen more than a few men die, stood with a worn, exhausted look on his face. Tears started to stream from his eyes when he saw me and the first thing he said was simply, "They got the Top, Bernie."

"I know, John," I murmured, looking away from his eyes. "I just had to identify his body at Graves Registration." He was the first of many.

"How'd they get him?" John had not seen the sergeant prior to him being evacuated in darkness the prior night.

I motioned with my finger to a point on my forehead just above and in the hairline.

"One shot, John. Right through the head."

(In retrospect, I'm not certain the Top was killed by a shot to the head, but that was how it appeared to me and I didn't want to tell John anything else at the time.)

Later, I was to learn that when they came under intense

enemy fire, the First Sergeant decided to move forward and assist his Company Commander. He was moving in a crouch, that ever present cigar clamped in his mouth, maneuvering his way through a world in chaos, firing occasionally, encouraging his boys to keep going but be careful, and he never heard the shot that killed him.

The last person I know of who spoke to the Top was the battalion commander, Lieutenant Colonel Trevor Swett, who landed his charlie-charlie to put John in the picture with regard to the tactical situation. Sergeant Hare had been the first soldier of the headquarters company for the 1/11th Infantry, the colonel's prior command; he and the Old Man were close. Twenty-five years later LTC Swett wrote:

"I saw Top Hare perhaps thirty minutes before he was killed. It was pouring rain and Bravo had just completed the lift from LZ English. John Hitti had already moved up to deploy the platoons and Top was getting things organized in the rear. I had to find John amidst the confusion and tell him what I knew. I got back to the charlie-charlie and we were about to lift off when a rain-shrouded figure gave me a thumbs-up from about fifty meters away. I recognized Top, (for some reason Top Hare and I always exchanged the thumbs-up sign), dismounted and ran over to see him. Rain was splashing on his nose and his cigar from the edge of his helmet. I remember saying, 'Watch your ass, Top,' and he replied, 'No sweat, Sir—Garry Owen'. A hand shake, a pat on the back, another thumbs up exchanged as my bird took off and the next time I saw him was in the morgue tent at LZ English."

First Sergeant Dayton L. Hare, Jr. was posthumously awarded his Combat Infantryman's Badge, the Purple Heart and the Silver Star for valor under fire. A short while later the officers and men of Company B made certain Mrs. Hare received that pattern of Noritake Ivory China.

I find it difficult to retell this account of Sergeant Hare without wondering about the vagaries of life. I cannot help thinking that under normal circumstances, I would have been at the rear of the company that day. Knowing me and the way I operated in subsequent fire fights, I would have probably gone forward to assist John Hitti. Except for being paymaster, I might have died and not the Top.

I believe Sergeant Major Robert Meyers decided that the First Sergeant should have some type of memorial erected in his memory. He had a very handsome metal plaque struck which commemorated Sergeant Hare by naming the battalion mess hall after him. The plaque, which measured perhaps fifteen inches square, stood on a three foot high cement pedestal in the center of the walkway up to the main doors of the mess.

I always went out of my way to enter the mess by the front door, in order to pass by the plaque. Invariably, I felt compelled to brush my hand across the metal on the way by, and I always asked quietly, "How's it going, Top?" Several times, late at night—when I was wrestling with some particularly difficult decisions and feeling isolated, as all officers do at times, or when I felt particularly down, having returned from the forward base after identifying a number of our dead—I would wander over to that modest monument and just stand there for a while, trying to figure out what The Top would say under the circumstances, if he were still alive. Invariably, I'd go away feeling better.

I have often wondered what happened to the plaque. I envision it having been thrown away by the South Viets when they took over the An Khe base late in the conflict; or, and more probable, knowing the poverty of the place, they melted down the metal for other uses. Certainly when the North Vietnamese swept over the camp, that remembrance would have been destroyed.

I hope they didn't melt it down. I like to think the stainless steel is still glinting in the sunlight amid the tall grasses and wild flowers somewhere near where the mess hall stood, defiant to the ravages of time and, in a sense, a symbol of victory over the country and the enemy Dayton Hare faced unafraid. Because occasionally, even twenty-eight years later, when life gets a little tough, I still find myself recalling the plaque and the man, and pausing to ask, "How's it going, Top?"

Memorial plaque to 1st Sergeant Dayton L. Hare, Camp Radcliff.

Chapter 4

Sergeant Nguyen

Sergeant Nguyen was Chinese. He was at pains to have us understand that. Vietnamese by nationality, perhaps by blood to some small degree, the consequence of intermarriage with ethnic Vietnamese over the generations—but Nguyen was Chinese, intrinsically. There was an observable sense of pride when he spoke of his origins. Chinese people were different, better that the ethnic Viets. He felt that way. To me the Chinese seemed more intense and more strongly motivated to do the correct thing. By that I mean Nguyen did everything he was asked without grumbling, without "a ration of shit thrown in", as the first sergeant would say.

Nguyen was our first interpreter. The sergeant dutifully showed up at our command post looking very apprehensive in his first assignment with an American unit. He gave Captain Hitti an uncertain salute, and announced quietly, in particularly good English, that he had been assigned to Bravo Company for the duration. I could appreciate Nguyen's feelings. He was presenting himself for duty with an American outfit. He would live, eat, work and perhaps die with these men who were complete strangers to him, to his country, and to its customs. I could just imagine myself being thrust into a Vietnamese line company, forever. That would be a tough assignment. The diet alone would have done me in.

In stature Nguyen could best be described as diminutive. The shortest American in the company had nearly half a foot on his five foot two inches. He couldn't have weighed more than one hundred pounds after a full meal, and lead in his pockets.

Nearly effeminate by our standards, with a dainty frame and finely sculptured face, soft voice and mild manner, with a very, very weak handshake, Nguyen was the antithesis of what an American would want in a military man. All our troops had seen the typical ARVN soldier in his tight fatigues, strolling along holding hands with another male soldier. Hand holding among men was accepted conduct in Southeast Asia and not synonymous with homosexuality, but our troops weren't quite sure of those guys. Nguyen, therefore, had a tough row to hoe. Surprisingly, however, he was liked and accepted almost at once. That was not just the result of Nguyen's hard work to prove himself as a capable soldier, but also the common sense and good leadership of John Hitti, who was uncommonly adept at making a new man feel a part of the unit.

John's first impression of the new interpreter was favorable. In private, he had a chat with Nguyen and the two hit it off nicely. John did reserve judgment until he saw Nguyen operate in the bush. He wanted to see if the ARVN could handle the tough going. He could.

What really pleased Nguyen no end, and made him thoroughly a part of the company, was when John issued him several sets of American jungle fatigues to replace his old ones. The jungle fatigues were superior for combat. They were lightweight and quick drying, so you didn't freeze at night in sweaty clothes. He also received a set of jungle boots which were far better than the leather ones he had. That was no easy trick, because Nguyen wore a size five. My boots looked like snow shoes in comparison. Warrant Officer Igoe, back in battalion supply, had to send an emergency requisition half way to hell for something

that small. And last but not least, the interpreter was issued his own M-16 to replace the M-2 carbine he carried.

The sergeant was good at what he did and good in a
fight. To top it all off, he had a sense of humor. I recall
the two of us scrunched behind a very small berm one day,
trying to avoid some enemy fire. The cover was barely
adequate and I was attempting to make my six foot, four
inch frame disappear when I heard Nguyen laugh and tell
me there were certain advantages to being his size. Just
then I certainly agreed.

Late in our tour, Nguyen unexpectedly presented himself in the personnel shop; he looked feverish and had a
deep cough that seemed to emanate from the very pit of
his lungs. I was the S-1 by that time and I asked him how
he was getting along and what I could do for him. He
responded by opening his shirt and showing me a large
reddish-purple bruise running the length of his breast bone.
It hurt. Aware there wasn't much medical expertise at the
ARVN compound in An Khe, he asked if I could have an
American doctor see him. I called the hospital, but unwit-
tingly made the mistake of saying Nguyen was Vietnamese.

"We don't treat gooks here," replied a sergeant.

I was livid and gave the sergeant a few choice words
which didn't impress him at all. I then worked up what
seemed an endless command ladder, but received the same
negative response, even from the top guy commanding the
outfit. Try as I might, there was no recourse, and I was
forced to send Nguyen to the ARVN doctors, such as they
were.

I have no idea what happened to Nguyen. He was a
brave and trusted comrade-at-arms who had fought with
us for nearly a year. At John Hitti's request, he had been
decorated with the United States Bronze Star Medal for
valor in combat. But to our medical people, in the words
of one, "Hell, man, he's just a gook." I think of him as
someone my army and I failed—another good man we used
and subsequently abandoned to the war and an uncertain
fate.

Chapter 5

Private Love's Traveling
Salvation Show

I first encountered him at Fort Carson. He was assigned to Bravo Company and was hard at work with all the others preparing to go to Vietnam. My initial notice was prompted by the comment of an old master sergeant with years of experience at assessing the qualities of recruits. The sergeant shook his head negatively while pointing to a group of troopers and said, "That man's never gonna make it, sir."

He was speaking about Love, Private Charles Love, who was always called just plain "Love", formally by the officers as protocol demanded, but, atypically, never Charlie or Chuck or Charles even by his close friends and barracks buddies. Private Love from the outset was clearly someone different.

A fair number of our troopers were country boys from West Virginia, Indiana, North Dakota; Love was from urban Denver, Colorado. The overwhelming majority of those farm boys were white. Love was black; but, in sharp contrast to the few black troopers we had who were all fairly tall and physically imposing, Charles Love was short, almost roly-poly, looked as wide as he was high, and about as ill-fit as you could be for the rigors of impending combat.

Another different thing about Love was that he always seemed to be smiling, even under the most adverse circumstances. One thoroughly nasty, rain and wind-filled night, I found him on guard detail. Every other soldier I'd seen up to that hour had on a miserable face, befitting the duty and the foul weather—not Love.

"How's it goin', Love," I asked?

Big smile.

"Just fine, Captain."

I'm tall and was more than just damp from the knees down where my rainwear failed to cover, so I added, "Tad wet out here tonight."

No big deal to Love. He simply went on to tell me how being on the short side allowed his poncho to keep him almost dry. No problem.

Not many days later, after a particularly strenuous physical training session, "How you doin', Love?"

Big smile.

"No sweat, sir. Garry Owen." I knew he was hurting.

In the company mess, "Food OK, Love?"

Big smile.

"Love it," he said, digging into an enormous portion of meat and potatoes. "Can't seem to lose any weight though." He never did.

Now, someone smarter than me once uttered the perverse military axiom that as long as your men are complaining about the chow, you don't have to worry about their morale—it's just fine. After Love praised the company mess, I thought I'd best speak to some other troopers and make sure we weren't in serious trouble. I did; they grumbled, chow was rotten, morale was fine.

Something you should understand about Love's smile — it was absolutely infectious; you were immediately compelled to smile in return. Since he was always smiling, he drove some of his NCOs crazy. Difficult to be serious with the guy when being serious was in order.

Love differed from every other man in the company in another very important respect. Love calmly announced one day that he was a reverend, a minister in his Denver church, as were his father and grandfather. Few believed him, but he persisted through a fair amount of good natured ribbing about being "his holiness". When you gave some thought to his claim, the man did have most of the qualities normally associated with a minister. He conspicuously got out a Bible every morning and started his day with verses and a prayer. Off-color jokes, bad language, arguments, fighting were never his trademarks. That smile and a good word were always there, no matter how foul the weather or onerous the duty. And someone neglected to give him the usual advice about volunteering. Need help? Love was apt to be the first to lend a hand.

Shortly after our arrival in South Vietnam, the mail brought to Love a copy of his church bulletin which was subsequently passed around in the company. Sure enough, The Reverend Charles Love was formally listed as one of the three Loves ministering in that church. By that time, however, few doubted that he was someone different and special; and being in a war didn't change him one bit, except that he seemed to suffer more when one of our men was injured or killed. Love's concern for his buddies was demonstrated the day we took our first KIA.

After working for some weeks along the South China Sea coast, Bravo Company was ordered to conduct a search and destroy operation in a heavily wooded, mountainous area west of Bong Son City. The air assault was uneventful, but we soon found that portions of the hill tops resembled one big punji pit. In some places, there were punji sticks in every tuft of grass and even embedded in the trunks of trees. We had three men wounded by them almost before the entire company got on the ground.

First Platoon, Love's unit, was given the mission to recon some high ground perhaps two thousand meters from our position. Attempting to avoid the punji sticks, they utilized a well worn path which ran along the spine of a steep ridge. All went well on the way to their objective, but they made the mistake of using the same trail on their return. Someone was watching their every move.

The booby trap was a metal can filled with nails and stones, backed with an explosive charge and detonator. The device was set in the ground at an angle and aimed up the trail toward the returning platoon. Obviously, it had not been there when they passed that same spot going out. The point man hit the trip wire, but was unhurt. The second man in line took multiple fragments in his legs only. Third man, the acting squad sergeant and a fine soldier, Specialist Fourth Class Frank P. Light, caught the charge right in his chest. We heard the explosion from the Company HQ. The platoon leader radioed he had a major problem and we mounted a small relief party and hurried to the scene. The necessity for prompt medical evacuation was immediately apparent, but there was no open area to accommodate a chopper, and we didn't think we could carry the critically wounded man back to our landing zone without inflicting more damage on him. A medevac with a hoist was requested, on the double.

While a life and death struggle ensued between Light and our medic, who was trying to keep Frank from drowning in his own blood, men with machetes, bayonets, any available tool were tearing at vines and trees, trying to open a hole in the green canopy about thirty feet overhead. The drama was unmatched in frantic activity, and I saw Love, in what seemed like a frenzy, trying with only his bare hands to pull down a tree which would eventually take the combined weight of half a dozen men to fell. Finally, an opening was made in the covering and a hovering chopper winched the wounded man through the small blue hole, using a special stretcher. We could see Frank still fighting for his breath and life half way up; then his head flopped to his chest and his body went limp. We all stood there, necks craned upwards, watching and hoping. I looked

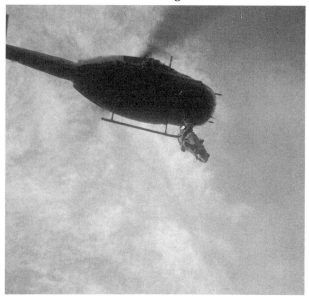

Frank Light, severely injured by a booby trap,
is hoisted to an evacuation chopper

around and saw Love on one knee, head bowed, praying. Minutes later, battalion reported that Frank Light was dead on arrival.

A dispirited cortege returned to the company command post. In my hands was Light's equipment; in my mind, senseless images:

I'm a teenager. John Wayne is portraying a Navy Seabee officer during World War II and his good friend has just been mortally wounded in a Japanese attack on a critical airfield. With the fate of the entire Pacific Theater hanging in the balance, The Duke, in starched and pressed khakis, dress cap and shoes, runs into the open through a cacophony of enemy machine gun and rifle fire. Grenades and artillery explode. Japanese bullets spurt puffs of dirt all around his feet, but he reaches his objective—a bulldozer which he throws in gear and, with the blade deflecting bullets, he destroys an enemy machine gun nest, miraculously causing the remainder of the Japanese forces to melt away. Our hero returns to his friend's side in time to see him smile and peacefully die of no visible causes.

John Wayne didn't die; the heroes never did. They could run through untold numbers of bullets and bombs unscathed. Some few buddies were lost, dropping slowly in their tracks when shot, and dying rather cleanly, without gasping for breath, never writhing in pain or agony.

However, now I am twenty-four years old and in the real world of 1966—Vietnam—Specialist Fourth Class Frank A. Light has, in fact, died. There was a bloody froth at his mouth; he couldn't breathe, drowning in his own fluids; a look of terror filled his face as he struggled against suffocation. A handsome, blond haired, blue eyed lad, very likable, SP/4 Light was not yet twenty. A booby trap got him—no hail of small arms fire, no glorious charge into the teeth of the enemy. Just a miserable tin can filled with rusty nails and stones which exploded into his chest. Ef-

Charlie Love (left) at An Khe, March 1967

forts to staunch the dreadful flow of frothy pink blood oozing from beneath the bandage covering the wound were in vain. He lived only a few more agonizing minutes while his buddies, few having ever witnessed death, let alone violent death, wondered in shock what the hell became of John Wayne.

I saw Love later that day. His eyes were moist and he seemed to be somewhere else.

"Love, how you doin'?"

No smile. "Just fine, Captain," he answered unenthusiastically.

Love went on with the rest of us. Bravo was involved in some very heavy fighting and he was there for the worst. If no chaplain was available on Sunday, Love would hold a service. Men in need of counsel would seek him out. He could always be counted on in any circumstance.

The last time I saw him in the field was late in our tour. I had been ordered to command a temporary radio relay station located on a hill in the wild bush country north of the Cav main base at An Khe. I flew in on an early resupply bird and was pleased to find Love in charge of one of the squads securing the place. Typically, even there, he was holding morning devotions. A small knot of men were gathered around him and that Bible he'd hauled with him the entire year.

I quietly joined the group for their final prayer and, as the men went about their duties, I asked, "How's it goin' my friend?"

We'd been through a long year. Only about half of the original battalion were still in action. After Light, we had seen too many men go down. A lifetime of rice paddies and mountain ridges had been crossed. Love was tired. He had that gaunt, dull-eyed look about him which betrays an exhaustion that can't be remedied by a night in a combat foxhole, no matter how long the sleep; but, with all that...

Big Smile.

"Great, Captain; just great."

Chapter 6

Friends Of The District Chief

The three looked nearly identical, dressed in old fatigues, leather boots, helmets without the camouflage cover, chin straps hanging loose. Because Nguyen, our interpreter, didn't come from the area, the Vietnamese District Chief decided we needed a few local military types to point out the Viet Cong, if we found any. We were assigned a sergeant and two PFCs from the 22nd ARVN Division who were supposed to be able to identify the good guys from the bad. Willy and Joe, as I came to think of them, were armed with M-1s. Their leader, Moe, had an M-2 carbine. They arrived lightly loaded, field packs nearly empty, expecting us to furnish all their meals. No problem. Moe quickly made it known that he was a very big toad in his particular puddle, in tight with the District Chief. We were unimpressed.

The friends of the District Chief were with us for several days, keeping to themselves for the most part. As we moved through villages and past farm huts, they would question any inhabitants found at home. The locals we found were all women, children or older men. A good deal of yelling and crying would come from those huts as these guys did their thing. They thought nothing of slapping the women around. Since my typical position in the line of march was Tail End Charlie, I was the first to recognize that these guys weren't out there to win hearts and minds, and I informed John Hitti. With Nguyen translating, the company commander informed them their modus operandi wasn't acceptable. Nothing good came from that lecture. Nguyen looked worried.

The ARVN always worked at the rear of the company and I had difficulty keeping track of them without assigning Nguyen to monitor their every move. Even then, the three would drift away from the formation to some huts that were off our line of march, or they would stay behind after we left a hamlet to finish their questioning of the locals. The ARVN honcho paid little heed to what we told him to do. He just smiled insincerely and went his own way. On their second full day with us, however, John specifically asked Nguyen to keep an eye on them; we noticed their field packs were filling up with something.

Day three, their packs were bulging. Near mid-afternoon, each of them came away from one farm hut with a live chicken held by the legs, wings flapping. They were expecting to feast that night. Behind them came one old mamma san raising hell. John and I, along with Nguyen, happened to be nearby as the trio emerged with the screaming woman in pursuit. When the ARVN honcho saw us, he tried to silence the old lady with a punch, but she was a lively old girl and he missed, thanks in part to the struggling fowl. John and I stepped into the middle of the fray. More women and ancient men materialized from the nearby hamlet to watch the confrontation. John asked Nguyen to question the woman. The mamma san, in a highly animated conversation punctuated by curses and comments from the ARVN sergeant, explained that she owned the chickens which she claimed the men confiscated without paying. Moe, not at all understanding the American sense of justice and fair play, didn't dispute her story, but simply explained to Nguyen that they were VC chickens. John gave the birds back to her and there were smiles all around among the populace. However, at that point a second

woman, emboldened by the victory of the first, stepped
forward from the crowd and claimed the trio had extorted
money from her and many others, threatening that we, the
Americans, would kill her and destroy the village if she
didn't hand the bandits all her cash. The ARVN sergeant
was clearly not a quick study; he hadn't learned any lesson
from his first loss. He countered to John, through Nguyen,
that the woman was VC, expecting that fact would be
reason enough for shaking down the entire village.

John Hitti had a particular way of getting mad. He
developed a look about him so intense that you had no
doubt he was furious. His face became red; his jaw tight-
ened; he fixed you in what only could be described as a
hate stare; his fists clenched involuntarily and his shoulders hunched up. The miscreants stood there with a grin
affixed to each of their faces as an obviously angered Hitti
started slowly toward them. The grin changed to a questioning, fearful look and they started to back away. The
trio all had their weapons slung over one shoulder. The
head man tried to grab for his carbine, but I got to his
free arm first. Several of our men quickly disarmed the
other two and we put them down, very hard and uncer-
emoniously, on their bellies, hands behind their backs. Their
packs disgorged candle sticks, watches, rings, a bolt of silk
cloth, a small portable radio, sandals and the like—a trea-
sure trove of valuables taken from the peasants we had
passed for the past three days. A search of the head man's
pockets revealed the watch that yet another woman claimed
they took and which he hadn't had time to add to the
collection in his rucksack. Since the bastard had three others
in the pack, there was little doubt about ownership, and
John returned the timepiece. Pockets and packs produced
over three thousand Vietnamese piasters, far too much
money to consider pocket change. Obviously, this was the
haul from shaking down every person they passed. The
ARVN sergeant, no smile on his face now, continued to
claim the swag was all Viet Cong money and, therefore,
rightful spoils of war. His logic was unimpressive. John
returned a portion to those villagers who claimed to have

been robbed by the trio.

Later that day we loaded the resupply chopper with the three of them trussed up like the bandits they were, their packs filled with the evidence of their theft. We had radioed ahead to our S-2, letting him know we wanted charges preferred against the lot. As I watched Willy, Joe and Moe depart, I knew inherently we were not destined to win the war. I didn't want to believe that truth, but I was thinking of a German proverb which postulated: a great war leaves the country with an army of cripples, an army of mourners, and an army of thieves. In Vietnam, the cripples and mourners were frequently evident, but my sense of the proverb had been that the thieves were Teutonic warriors plundering on foreign soil. In significant contrast, the three ARVN pillagers had victimized their own people. How, I wondered, can any war be won with thieves for allies? Clearly, this so-called people's war could never be decided in our favor with friends of the District Chief looting the district.

CPT John Hitti using PRC 25 radio, with Vietnamese farm family in Binh Dinh Province

Chapter 7

Hard Luck Charlie

You didn't want to get too close to Jon Charles Merton. He preferred Charlie, or Chas, over Jon. We just called him Hard-Luck Charlie. The problem was that Charlie was visited with so many calamities, minor and major, one received the impression the gods had an interest in making him a modern-day Job. If someone was going to get a monumental case of diarrhea from taking his malaria pills, the guy would be Chas. When a disoriented, chopper flight leader deposited one of our units in the wrong LZ, it was apt to be Charlie's Platoon.

Typical of Lieutenant Merton's terrible luck is the fact that he may have commanded the only unit in Vietnam to be attacked by a tiger. That is correct, a tiger—or something like that.

At the time, Bravo Company was guarding the bridges of Highway 19. Charlie had strategically placed his men at bridges and isolated strong points in an effort to keep the Viet Cong from any mischief. Being a good platoon leader, he was rotating between his positions. The tiger picked the one he was visiting, and did so about two in the morning while the lieutenant was conferring with Morpheus.

In fairness, the night was very dark and we had been in-country only a few weeks. So, when one defensive position cut loose with an M-16 on full automatic, there was no wonder that, before the lieutenant regained control, every man had blown off at least four clips of ammunition which sounded, in Chas' words, "like a small, dag-gone war out there".

Truly, it was quite a racket, accompanied by several illuminating rounds, all of which could be heard and seen from company headquarters. John Hitti wanted to know what was happening, and Charlie, in the heat of the action (all outgoing, but he hadn't figured that out yet), told the captain he was under attack. Only later did he discover that his men, according to the PFC who started the whole thing, were shooting at "a tiger, Lieutenant; swear to God—ah, or somethin' like that—actually it looked like a black cat." The creature was of no small proportions, naturally, glimpsed creeping toward the perimeter.

The problem with all this was that John had already notified battalion and was mounting a relief patrol to go to Charlie's aid when the call came in that the attack was just a mistake. I wasn't around when Chas explained that one to the good captain, but could easily imagine the consternation when the explanation went back up the chain of command: "Actually, Colonel, it was—ah—a large black cat—or something like that."

In addition to Charlie's propensity for trouble, there were tongue-in-cheek discussions concerning the possibility that the lieutenant's metabolism might be creating an electromagnetic field around him which drew pieces of metal to his body. If any metallic objects were flying anywhere in his vicinity, one of them would hit Lieutenant Merton. You really wanted to keep clear of the guy when there was contact with the enemy. Charlie held the battalion record for being wounded—four separate times.

The most comical disaster that befell Lieutenant Merton happened at an artillery fire base. The artillery battery sported huge, 8-inch, self propelled guns. They had established a defensive perimeter encircling a low, very small hill. The guns were on the western side of the hill and our company HQ was set up on the eastern side.

On the top of the rise, opposite the artillery pieces, was a very nicely built bunker. The edifice was roomy, made completely of sandbags up to a level of about four feet, and had a nice sleeping platform built in. All this home away from home lacked was a roof and, best of all, it was not occupied when our lieutenant happened along. Chas assumed this stroke of good fortune had been abandoned by the infantry unit we were replacing. He took possession by rigging his poncho over the top in tent-like fashion. The bunker was very comfortable, indeed. I recall peering in there that first night and seeing him at his nightly ritual of writing a letter to his wife. He constructed a desk from several ammunition crates and was sitting on another. Two candles on either side of his writing materials were lighting the interior gloom, making the desk look like an altar. Chas was happy.

Now when we arrived, the artillery battery was pointed generally west. They were giant guns mounted on track vehicles about the size of a tank, with the throat of the cannon projecting beyond the front of the vehicle. Throughout the day we would hear the artillerymen yell "Fire Mission", and the engines powering the tracks would crank up and move the gun in the general direction they were to fire. There were then a few seconds while the gunners adjusted the tubes in response to commands from their Fire Direction Center. The weapon was much too large to adjust by hand; therefore, fine adjustments in elevation and deflection were accomplished by small electric motors which could be heard going on and off with a whining sound. At the command, "Fire", the gun would discharge.

We quickly became accustomed to that pattern. The roar of the guns was bothersome, but they were firing generally west and the sound tended to travel away from us.

At dusk on the third night we were there, I stopped by Charlie's hooch and found him set up as before with his writing paper and candles.

"Another letter to the little woman?" I inquired.

"Hell yes," was his reply. (He normally preceded most answers requiring a simple yes with the word hell, pronounced in what was, I guess, an Oklahoma accent, making the response sound more like, "Hail yass.")

He was dressed in undershorts, T-shirt, and unlaced combat boots only. His clothes were hung from a post supporting the poncho roof. His bed was all set up with his poncho liner neatly laid out. To one side was a makeshift table on which all his shaving gear and toilet articles were arranged. He had a styrofoam cup filled with hot coffee and all his writing gear and paper on his desk in front of him, scribbling away.

I started down to the artillery mess truck which was still serving coffee. I heard "Fire Mission" yelled from the artillery fire direction center and, as I approached the mess area, a gleeful mob of artillerymen were gathering as if something special was about to happen. They were all looking back toward Charlie's hooch, and only then did I understand why that nice, well-built, sandbag mansion had been vacant. The 8-inch gun closest to the hill was then slowly turning from a westerly direction to the east. Its position was at the base of that very small hill. In fact, a part of the hillside had been chopped out to provide a firing position. When the gun stopped turning, the muzzle, which to that point in time was forty feet from Charlie's hooch and pointing in the opposite direction, was now only about twenty feet away at best and aimed to fire directly over the top of the hill and Hard Luck Charlie's poncho.

"Wait 'till you see this," said a smiling artillery sergeant standing beside me, scarcely able to conceal his amusement.

"Zero, one, niner," the gun sergeant was shouting numbers for the crew to adjust to the target and the whine of the electric motors was heard briefly as the gun muzzle moved almost imperceptibly.

"Fire," yelled the gun sergeant, shortly after the motors stopped.

BAMM—the discharge, and in an instant the tremendous muzzle blast which could send its giant projectile twenty thousand kilometers, seemed to collect beneath Charlie's poncho, bulging the fabric outward as it strained at the tie-down ropes, then ripping the poncho roof off the hooch and propelling it, letters, writing paper, clothing, shaving gear, poncho liner, coffee, dirt, stones, sticks and anything else that was loose, down slope. This blizzard of equipment and papers was followed almost instantaneously by Charles Merton, clumsily running in those unlaced boots as if shod with snowshoes.

The blast did get everyone's attention. Faces cautiously emerged from bunkers to see if we'd been hit by a rocket. They observed artillerymen in a fit of glee, a snowstorm of Charlie's love letters and writing materials fluttering to earth, and the lieutenant fleeing as if the demons of hell were in pursuit.

John Hitti managed to get him stopped or he might have gone right through the barbed wire and be running today. I can't describe how funny those artillery boys thought the event was. They were standing around with tears of laughter in their eyes and, to tell the truth, I was laughing right along.

After gathering his belongings, Chas bunked in with the CO for the night. I visited later. He was still composing to his wife.

"You survive, old man?" I asked.

Without missing a letter, "Hail yass."

Chapter 8

The Statistic

The boy looked perhaps twelve years old. He was average in height as kids in Vietnam go, with bright, white teeth and short, black hair which had been freshly cut by his mother, or someone else equally unskilled at the task. The boy was typically dressed for a youngster, in nothing but a pair of boxer shorts which may once have been white, but were now a dingy gray. He was really just a child, a very frightened child who was crying quietly.

When I happened along, the lad was in the rough grasp of Specialist Fourth Class Vincente "Poncho" Villa, a member of our First Platoon. Poncho had a painfully firm hold on the upper arm of the boy who, with stiff and unbending legs, was obviously coming along involuntarily from the group of hooches to our rear. Periodically the boy would glance furtively upward at the big soldier with a "where-are-you-taking me" look on his face.

Villa muscled the boy to the water's edge where members of the platoon's point fire team were crouched behind some trees and stumps, forced him down the short embankment, and shoved him into the black, murky liquid. The boy sank into the mud below the water and, in response to the soldier's push, involuntarily took a stumbling step or two, trying to regain his balance. He was quickly up to his chest and turned, peering questioningly at the men who gestured for him to go to the copse. The boy looked out into the swamp and started to cry in earnest, shaking his head negatively, seeming to comprehend what the men wanted. He started back up the embankment, but Villa took a threatening step toward him and the frightened boy turned and hesitatingly started out into the black water, crying loudly.

First Platoon was stalled. The day had been yet another running battle with snipers in the mangrove swamps along the South China Sea. At one point our men were forced to use a single, very low dike running out from a fishing village, traversing several hundred meters of open water to their final objective for the day. Impeding their progress, however, was a mangrove copse with a commanding field of fire over the dike on which they must advance. The tangle of grey-black mangrove roots and waxy green leaves forming that particular stand of low trees was exceptionally thick; it appeared to be a tiny dry island just fifteen or so feet across, into which the fire team had pumped a mass of small-arms rounds. That fusillade left much of the vegetation facing us shredded or broken.

Several of the men were certain they saw movement in the tangle, certain that sniper fire had come from that general direction. They were concerned a guerrilla could have ducked under the roots into the water and avoided our bullets. He could be swimming underwater away from us now, or he could be waiting for the team to get into the open. No one was willing to venture out on that dike until they make certain nothing nasty was in the copse. Assaulting through the open water could invite big trouble. They had a stalemate until Villa produced the boy. He would go out there and we'd see what happened.

The journey for the boy was an endless forty meters. Halfway there, he turned again to retreat, looking with tear-filled eyes and stained cheeks at the men on shore, one of whom pointed a gun at him and motioned for him to continue his journey. Reluctantly, obviously nearly sick with fear, he did, crying all the more.

We were suspicious. The kid was the son of a fisherman. Doubtless the water itself was not causing him to be so dramatically fearful. At his age he would have been fishing with his father for years; the rivers and ocean would have been his second home. No, the lad was aware of something to be very afraid of in that mangrove tangle. As he struggled closer, the fire team became more tense; thumbs flicked the safety off weapons; trouble, if there was to be any, was about to happen.

As he approached within ten feet of the copse, the boy hesitated yet again and cried louder. One of the men gestured menacingly with his M-16. The boy, then beyond himself with fear, moved closer to the thicket and reached in, only to withdraw his hand quickly as if struck by a snake. He was screaming hysterically and wheeled around to leave. The man who took him from his village and forced him into the water fired a shot in his direction, sending a geyser of water into the air to his left. The boy returned to the copse. He was shaking, crying, sniffling and choking from the tears and mucus running out his nose and down his throat. He looked back at the men once more, reached in the tangle and grasped something with one hand, then with two, as he struggled to pull it free. Throughout the process he continued a fearful, crying scream, trying to get the terrifying object dislodged. The thing suddenly released; the boy lost his footing and fell backward, his head disappearing beneath the surface only to bob up quickly, choking, sputtering, screaming. He gingerly grasped the object, which was semibuoyant and floating just beneath the surface, and started for shore; but one of the men stopped him with a shout and pointed to his gun and to the mangroves, making the lad understand that he wanted any weapons that could be found in the tangle. The boy returned and looked in, but apparently saw nothing. Then with great effort in that chest deep muck and water, he dragged the object behind him to the shore and ran off to the huts, screaming as if he had been wounded to the quick.

The object was a woman's body, or most of it; a good portion of her head was blown away. Villa hefted her partially out of the water. There was just a great empty cavity where the brain once resided, another testament to the tremendous destructive force of the M-16 rifle. Apparently, one round entered the top of her head as she lay prone in the thicket and blew out the lower, back half of her skull. Death was instantaneous.

The woman didn't resemble the local ladies. She appeared to have been well-fed, solid looking, not thin as were most of the women in that area. Someone suggested she was taller than the locals, lighter complexioned. Her water soaked blouse clung to her, causing her nipples to stand out and reveal full, well-formed breasts. We judged her to be about thirty. The woman's face was unmarked except that her jaws seem clenched, locked in a perpetual grimace, suggesting she knew the bullets were flying towards her, perhaps hoping they'd miss, knowing they probably wouldn't.

We wondered aloud who this person was. Why was she in the copse? There was no reason to conceal herself unless she was, in fact, the enemy. The local mamma sans didn't hide from us. And why was the boy so terrified? He undoubtedly knew someone was out there, someone of whom he was very frightened. She may have been with the North Vietnamese Army advising the Viet Cong. That was the conventional wisdom. We'll never know. She had no documents. The report of "One KIA, suspected NVA advisor, female, no weapon, no documents" was radioed to the Battalion S-2.

Using his boot, one of the men pushed the body back into the water where it partially disappeared from sight, sinking feet first until only a mass of long black hair was visible on the surface, the strands parting occasionally in the eddying currents to reveal, indistinctly, her face.

There was a hush among the men as they gathered their

gear almost without a word, an involuntary respectful silence in the presence of the dead. Poncho looked once more down the embankment toward the body, but what was once a human being had completely disappeared; only the drag marks in the mud remained. His face seemed to reveal an inner sorrow, frustration and consternation. His "Let's move out-" was said in a resigned, whispered exhale as if he were trying to expel the woman from his mind, but knowing he'd remember her. The point fire team started cautiously across the dike.

I seldom saw a Vietnamese woman I considered attractive. They always looked so old and worn before their time. That woman, however, would have been very pleasant to look at, I think. Standing there watching the body sink into the water, I can remember being struck with sadness at the waste of that beauty, that human person. However, we returned to business as usual, and we counted one more body for the boys wearing the stars and eagles. She became just another scratch mark on a pad of paper, another numeral which, when added to all the others, would eventually "prove" we were winning the conflict. She would be yet another statistic which, if you believed them, would eventually add up to our having killed nearly an entire generation of North Vietnamese. However, there is one you can believe. A human being—sex, female; name, unknown; address, unknown; occupation, unknown; resting place, uncertain—was dead, absolutely, forever. Those unknowns and the woman herself seemed to be a personification of the war. She was dead, but we weren't certain exactly who among us killed her, if we did, or why we did, because we don't know if she was the enemy at all or just a noncombatant who panicked and tried to hide. I know one thing, however. The statistics of the dead and the wounded missed one innocent victim—the boy. I am certain he was scarred for life by that event.

Chapter 9

Shades Of Cornelius Vane

Affecting a manner steeped in sincerity, the battalion surgeon announced emphatically, "I can't go out there. I get sick, air sick." His naturally squeaky voice assumed an excited tone and rose an octave as he continued, "and besides, what if we got shot down? What if I got killed?" His always helmeted head was shaking negatively, a worried expression was on his face. "That would be a much greater loss than if any one of them died," he added, gesturing almost derisively toward a squad of weary looking, dust covered soldiers trudging by. "With my medical training and background, my loss would be greater than if—ah—let's say—ah—even you died, captain."

He wasn't kidding. The son of a bitch was looking me square in the eye and explaining that the world would be better off if I bought the farm or if one of those troopers died rather than him. Matter-of-factly he said it, almost condescendingly, as if he were a father simply explaining the facts of life to a child.

I'm certain I must have been grinning stupidly at him, a sort of you're-putting-me-on expression on my face, and then I blurted out a nervous laugh. I really didn't take him seriously at first, didn't want to. However, as he continued, the truth sank into my disbelieving brain. He meant exactly what he said, and now it seemed he was compelled to justify this social triage with a recitation of his lineage—from a long line of professionals, best schools, but had to struggle for the degree. Therefore, his survival was particularly essential.

"Thank you, Doctor," I said as I walked away, mockingly polite and placing a heavy emphasis on the "doctor". I believe the sarcasm escaped him.

The companies in the field were losing too many men to sickness and other ailments. The recent weather had been rotten, and to make matters worse, the battalion was operating in an area of flooded rice paddies. The company medics couldn't do much in the way of medical treatment, their forte being trauma wounds—they didn't have the know-how or the supplies. Therefore, I had simply suggested to the doc, who was not really a surgeon but a general practitioner, that a little preventive medicine in the form of his visiting the troops in the field might keep some of those guys off of sick call, might make life just a little easier for them. By his response, you would have thought I asked him to lead the Charge of the Light Brigade instead of taking a few short helicopter rides.

Our first battalion surgeon, the man who deployed with us from Fort Carson, seemed to enjoy getting out with the troops. Once, while flying with the Old Man, the two of them landed in the midst of a fire fight and the doc was able to help one trooper who had a serious belly wound. Unfortunately, that fellow's skills were needed elsewhere and we got this new guy who wouldn't fly.

The word was that the doc had been blessed with a "profile"—military parlance for a physical disability which impaired one's performance, or, and more descriptive of this doctor, a medical problem which limited the duties he could be required to undertake.

Physically, our doctor certainly didn't appear to be unfit for anything. He stood about six feet tall, no flab, a lean and mean type. He smiled frequently, always kept himself spotless, and obviously thought well of himself. His helmet was tilted ever so slightly at a rakish angle, never was he without a holstered pistol and, even in the heat of the tropics, was often seen with a green ascot at his neck. The doc cut quite a physically fit, military figure.

There we were, however, in the First Cavalry Division, Airmobile. That is correct, Airmobile—four-hundred-odd helicopters and fixed wing aircraft assigned to the Division—and this doctor has a profile; the dude can't fly. Or, more precisely, he can't fly in helicopters. Fixed wing aircraft which get up above the reasonable possibility of being shot down seemed to be fine. He managed to gut them out since those were the only transport between Landing Zone English and An Khe, unless you wanted to ride in an open jeep along some very dangerous roads. Yes, the high flying aircraft seemed acceptable, but those low flying birds made him sick.

I hadn't gotten more than a few yards from my encounter with Captain Courageous when I heard him shouting orders to some troops engaged in filling sandbags. Technically, those guys were all sick and assigned to light-duty, yet they represented a work force for him. A trooper reports for sick call and if he is not too ill, he's put on temporary light-duty at the LZ until his minor ailment clears up. His duties while in that status are controlled by the doctor. The guys he was shouting at were hard at work reconstructing a portion of the battalion surgeon's private quarters, a bunker they had christened "the tomb".

The doc had given me the grand tour of that structure. He had a circular hole, perhaps ten feet in diameter, dug three feet into the ground. A sandbag wall, two feet thick and four feet high, was then built completely around the perimeter of the cavity. Three small openings, which could be closed off with sandbags, were placed in the wall facing north, east and west, and served for ventilation. The entire structure was roofed over with heavy, interlocking, pierced steel planks, the kind the Combat Engineers made aircraft runways with, and was topped with three layers of sandbags. The opening into this edifice jutted from the south wall and looked a bit like the entrance to a lumpy, olive green, flat-topped igloo. It was much lower than the bunker's roof, obliging one to assume a rather undignified position and back into it on hands and knees, down two steps, and drop feet first to the floor. The entrance could also be closed off with sandbags. There was little doubt the tomb could take a near miss from a substantial explosive round without harm to its lone occupant.

However, what if the Viet Cong overran the camp? His answer was to build, against one inside wall of the tomb, a bunker within a bunker which took the form of a raised platform about three feet high and eight feet long, made of sandbags. Roofed with steel plank and a layer of bags, and with his air mattress draped with a mosquito netting on top, the whole affair looked to all the world like a solid sleeping platform; but, in reality, it could be entered from one end by removing sandbags and crawling inside. With the bags replaced, the hidden occupant was doubly protected. The troops who constructed that little gem dubbed it "the coffin".

That day he was directing the last phase of construction on this masterpiece built by a man so concerned about his survival and, in reality, so frightened, I reasoned that if an attack ever did come, he wouldn't be able to pull himself together enough to use those clever facilities.

More germane to his reason for being there at all, of course, was the question of just what the doctor's duties were in the event we were attacked. Infantrymen like myself would have preferred the battalion surgeon be at his post in the medical tent, available to anyone who was wounded fighting off the enemy and concomitantly defending him. (Make no mistake, that first aid tent was also heavily sandbagged. Being very large, it lacked overhead cover, but was in the center of our battalion area, very well defended, and protected from all but high-angle enemy fire.) But all those bunker preparations led me to the worrisome conclusion that our medical guy would be hunkered down in his burrow, as opposed to being at his duty station. We found out the night Landing Zone English exploded.

LZ English was the Cav's forward, combat support base at the time. The facility covered thousands of acres, with an airstrip capable of accommodating C-130 cargo aircraft. To support major operations, a mammoth ammunition dump was located there. One June night in 1967, the dump exploded with a roar, the repeat of which I've yet to experience in any form, nor do I wish to.

We were located nearly half a mile away from the ammunition facility, but everyone felt the initial blast and were witness the rest of the night to a titanic display of violence. For five hours a significant portion of the horizon was lighted angry shades of red, white, and yellow so continuously bright, I had no difficulty reading the hands of my watch. Thousands of tons of explosives went off, one detonation seeming to ignite the next. At times you could hear individual shells exploding, then tons would erupt in a single gigantic roar, shaking the earth. Even at that distance we could feel the concussion and occasionally the heat of the blasts. Phosphorus streamers were arcing through the sky and pieces of burning shell curlicued out of the inferno. Huge billows of yellowish white and black smoke blew off to the East toward the South China Sea. The burning explosives smelled as I imagined Dante's hell would.

For a time I stood outside our tactical operations center, watching with the chaplain and several others. Everyone was nearly transfixed by the sheer magnitude of the violence before us; but, gradually, we came to the realization, when the din diminished periodically, that there was a kind of intermittent tinkling sound all about us—a gentle, not unpleasant noise almost like the falling of an icy snow, mixed occasionally with a sound akin to small hailstones striking frozen ground. We soon understood the source of the sounds. Bits and pieces of steel and aluminum, tiny fragments of the exploding ammunition, were raining all about us. When one in our company noted that several of the pieces landed with quite a thud, and retrieved a piece weighing a pound or more, prudence dictated we seek shelter and put the word out for everyone to get under some overhead cover.

With the daylight, we found that scarcely a tent didn't have several jagged holes in the fabric from the heavier of the falling debris; and the roofs of our sandbagged bunkers and the ground all about were littered with pieces of mortar tail assemblies, empty cartridge casings, shell fragments of every description, and even entire artillery rounds which had failed to explode.

Early that morning, when daylight had arrived, several of the mess sergeant's finest were at work mixing pancake batter, making coffee and generally preparing to serve breakfast. Although the dump was still exploding periodically, sending a cloud of black smoke into an otherwise pristine sky, the falling objects had ceased, or so we thought. I was in the mess tent very early, shooting the breeze with the two cooks. Those fellows were already drenched in sweat, despite the relatively cool morning, having dressed

Explosion of the ammo dump at LZ English

themselves in their armored flak vests and steel helmets. Knowing my affinity for hot cakes, a preview batch had been started and were about half done when a swoosh was heard, followed by a clank and a dull thud as something hit the ground. The three of us looked in shock at a foot-long, four inch wide, jagged piece of shell which had fallen through the tent top and landed in the narrow gap between the two stoves they were using, putting a murderous dent in the side of one of them. The object must have weighed three pounds or more, and was still too hot to hold. Had its trajectory been two feet further to either side we'd have lost a cook, a bit shorter on its flight and I would have been wearing it. The cooks needed no order to exit the mess posthaste, not to be seen until all explosions had ceased for good.

I am almost ashamed to say it, but after a time in combat I'm afraid one developed the tendency to become a bit numb to danger. I do not attribute that reaction to bravery; the word reckless may better describe the attitude. Therefore, reasoning that lightning was not about to strike in the same spot twice, I took up a spatula and rescued the pancakes, with the obvious in mind, only to be interrupted by a yell from the medical area not far away.

Specialist Four Bill Thorpe was calling for me. Earlier that day, he and another trooper from the supply section had taken it on themselves to drive a truck toward the center of the LZ and the ammo dump to see if they could be of help to anyone. They returned describing a scene of utter destruction and few people, although they did note that the perimeter was fully manned. All of the facilities near the dump were destroyed and abandoned at that early hour. Later we were to see that the evac hospital, which some genius had located immediately adjacent to the ammunition, was gone, utterly. So complete was the destruction that the refrigerated truck trailer belonging to the Graves Registration Unit had melted from the intense heat. Fortunately, some knowledgeable soldier had insisted the hospital staff have very good protective bunkers with overhead cover into which they dove when the first bang went off. They were rescued at the height of the inferno when two heroic armored personnel carrier crews drove into what must have appeared the mouth of hell, backed up to each bunker, and opened the carrier's rear hatch door, allowing the medical people to scramble safely inside.

After relating what he had seen, Thorpe led me to the rear of his truck. Prone on the cargo bed floor was a body. The corpse was an American soldier who appeared to have been in the wrong place at the wrong time, with no helmet, when a piece of falling steel fell back to earth.

"Picked him up just off the road, Sir," Thorpe said quietly. "I'm sure he's bought it, but I thought the doc ought to at least have a look at him."

The standard procedure called for dead men to be taken to the Graves Registration Unit at the hospital. However, with Thorpe's description of the evac hospital area, I thought there was no way we were going to find a doctor down there to declare this fellow dead, so I reasoned our man had a job to do.

I turned to several medical specialists standing nearby and asked, "Where's the doctor?"

With a rather embarrassed, eyes-to-the-ground look, one responded, "In the tomb."

Puzzled, I went over to the opening of the doctor's bunker and yelled inside for him, but received no answer. As I turned and crawled backward into the igloo entrance, I noted the medical troops had rather dejected looks on their faces.

The tomb was dimly lighted by what little sun was coming in the door. The windows were sandbagged closed. Having received no response from him, I expected to find the doctor asleep or possibly in the coffin, since he no doubt thought the LZ was in jeopardy. But as my senses adjusted to the gloom, I saw his body on the floor. He was fully clothed and clad in his armored vest, helmet and pistol. He was drawn up in a tight fetal position on his left side, knees nearly to his chin, with his hands gripping the edges of his steel pot, apparently trying to pull it down over his entire head. He was shaking. Lord, was he shaking. Every muscle in his body appeared to be aquiver and had been for some time, judging from the grooves the soles of his boots had rubbed into the hard dirt floor.

"Doctor, it's me, Captain Grady," I said in a hoarse whisper.

The shaking continued, unabated, as if he wasn't aware of my presence. Could he have been this way all night? I reached down and shook him, still attempting to make him understand who I was. He continued to tremble violently. Then I realized why his men looked so embarrassed. No doubt they had been in here trying to rouse him, also without success.

"Pull yourself together, Doc. Everything is fine outside, no VC attack, just the ammo dump blowing up," I said to him as I knelt on one knee with my hand on his shoulder. No luck. He still shook. It was absolutely unbelievable.

My patience started to wear thin. Some poor bastard was lying outside with half his head caved in, probably doing his duty when the end came, and here is this goddamned doctor, too good for the common man, frightened literally out of his senses at a moment when the worst of the situation had long since passed. He hadn't been scratched and wasn't about to be. What if one of those cooks, or I, had caught that fragment which nearly ruined my pancakes? Suppose someone had been injured earlier in the night? We probably would have died for lack of help while this worthless medicine man panicked.

Recalling my Ranger training about how to make a person hurt, I aimed a vicious kick at the top of his foot along the boot laces. The force of the blow with my combat boot brought a howl of pain, and an immediate cessation to the shaking. The doctor adjusted his helmet upward, opened his eyes and peered out from under its brim with a look of disbelief on his face as he realized, apparently, that he had been deliberately kicked.

"Get your miserable ass up and yourself together, Doctor. The LZ is quite safe," I said in the most sarcastic, forceful voice I could muster. "You are not going to die today." Lowering my voice to a conspiratorial whisper while pausing for a moment to allow the meaning to sink in to his fright paralyzed brain, I continued, "I have an injured man outside. You WILL get your worthless butt out there and you WILL look at him in the next thirty seconds, or else." I left the bunker without waiting for a response and without the least idea what my "or else" would be.

I presume the doctor surmised he was now faced with a more immediate, albeit unspecific, danger. He quickly appeared at the door of the bunker and stretched as if he had been asleep. He was quite an actor. Saying good morning to the assembled troops, he examined the prostrate form and quickly pronounced the man dead. The fraud seemed to be in control again. I was relieved; his own men appeared to be also.

Unfortunately, as he finished his examination, there was a low rumble from the ammunition dump. The noise wasn't very loud or threatening because I didn't duck, but the doctor, with a moan of terror, made an undignified scuttle to his bunker, the last few feet on hands and knees, and plunged in head first. The troops who saw him disappear turned and left, disgusted.

"Come on, Thorpe," I said, covering the remains with a piece of a tarp, "let's get this man on his way home."

As Thorpe and I carefully negotiated the litter strewn road toward the center of the landing zone in an attempt to locate the Graves Registration Unit, I was deep in thought.

Bill broke into my preoccupation. "What are you thinking about, Captain?"

"Cornelius Vane," I answered.

"Don't believe I know him."

"A poem, Bill—World War I—'The Execution of Cornelius Vane' by a guy named Herbert Read, I believe. The lines I recall go like this: 'I did not discover I was brave until I had sheltered in a ditch with a coward'."

With an expression that was a cross between disgust and sadness, "Yea," was Thorpe's only response.

Chapter 10

A Nice Walk To The Vinh Nuc Ngot

Bravo Company was struggling towards the sea. The rice paddy terrain had given way to much deeper water. Our objective was the Vinh Nuc Ngot, a large, salt water inland lake perhaps ten kilometers long and three wide.

"A nice walk in the sun," suggested the first sergeant wryly.

The day was a sensory pastiche. A cool breeze off the South China Sea was a refreshing change to the heat of past days. The smell of salt and sand evoked memories of much more pleasant, youthful times at the ocean side. An evening rain had rinsed the dust from the flora, enhancing their greens and browns, reds and yellows. As we waded acros a stretch of open water, the intense sunlight reflected off the ripples, creating a painful glare which significantly impaired our vision. The crump of impacting artillery sounded in the distance.

I was following a young fire team leader named Tom Binks. With my height, the water came just above my waist, but Tom was submerged nearly to his arm pits. He waded along with his rifle held over his head. Two packs of smokes, a nearly empty roll of toilet paper, and a small packet of papers and pictures wrapped in plastic were tucked into the elastic camouflage band of his helmet, in an attempt to keep those precious possessions dry. Unexpectedly, I saw him stagger backward, off balance. Regaining his footing, he rose on tip toes, staring intently into the shimmering surface immediately in front of him. Then, slowly, deliberately bringing his M-16 high over his head, he pulled the trigger with his thumb, directing a single round into the water no more than three feet ahead. The discharge resulted in a surprisingly large geyser. Tommy staggered backward, off balance again from the awkward manner in which he fired his weapon. Still, nothing was to be seen in the water except for the ripples radiating from the spot where the round struck the surface.

John Hitti had been on Binks' left and didn't see the episode unfold. I hardly need say the rifle shot surprised the you know what out of our company commander. He thought we had taken a sniper round. For his part, Tom lurched forward holding his rifle aloft, and reached down into the murk. His arm disappeared to his shoulder as he groped for something. He had a very serious look on his face. Shortly, he braced his feet and pulled upward, partially exposing the limp torso of a uniformed Vietnamese man. Tom Binks looked relieved.

A search of the bottom for the man's weapon, using our feet to sift through the muck, yielded an SKS assault rifle. Tom said the Vietnamese swam into him underwater, otherwise he wouldn't have known the man was there. The VC must have been breathing through a hollow reed because no one noticed him surface for air. Tom and I dragged the corpse to a nearby dike where we took some soggy papers from his pockets. He was uniformed, but not as an NVA soldier. We surmised he was a Viet Cong, Main Force guerrilla. The M-16 round had taken off the back of his skull; he never knew what hit him. The documents went to Division Intelligence. The SKS was Tom's. The body we committed back to the water.

Not long thereafter, the call went out for a medic, and Ron "Red Dog" Gow hustled over to a dike several hundred meters away. There, some of our men had discovered another uniformed Viet Cong, wounded but still alive. Red Dog returned a short while later with more papers, no weapon. The man had received an obviously terminal wound. The Doc could do nothing for him.

Nearing the sea, the terrain consisted of tidal swamp and marsh. Fishing villages shaded by the ever present coconut palm trees were located on some of the higher ground.

Bill Kail's Second Platoon had been ducking sniper fire, some of which was thought to have originated from a tiny hamlet which his men entered with nervous trigger fingers. There were civilians in the village and a number of young males were among them. Our men were lining up the Viets prior to searching the place when someone noticed a bush move and saw a hand come out of the ground beneath it. He fired and hit the hand. A young man was pulled from an expertly camouflaged spider hole. Apparently, the unfortunate gent didn't like how the bush was positioned and reached up to make adjustments at exactly the wrong moment, with disastrous results.

When Bill and I arrived, the wounded man was hunkered down on his haunches, grasping his left wrist with such force that the knuckles on the grasping hand were completely white, trying without much apparent success to end the pain. He was hit by the M-16 round on the knuckles of his left hand. The velocity of the round tore off three fingers, leaving only the thumb, his little finger, and a crescent of mangled, bloody flesh and shattered bone. He was in shock, quivering uncontrollably, face contorted in agony. There wasn't much blood, but the medic slipped a tourniquet around the man's wrist in the event some bleeding should develop.

The man was walked to the rear where the first sergeant was coordinating medevacs. The choppers were busy elsewhere. Someone at division decided a VC with a hand wound was low priority. He would wait hours for a resupply bird.

Our advance was delayed while the Doc went to take care of someone in a hut on the edge of the hamlet. He was nearly dragged there by an elderly woman I noticed had been observing him care for the wounded man. Not long after, the cry of a baby was heard and a smiling medic returned.

"First one I've ever helped deliver," he said, obviously pleased.

Shortly thereafter the terrain changed again, to sand. We walked one hundred meters or so, gradually uphill, in an area covered with low brush and shaded by palms. Topping that rise, we found ourselves face to face with the Vinh Nuc Ngot just a stone's throw beyond. Across the water was the Hung Lac Peninsula shimmering in the afternoon heat. The scene looked for all the world like an advertisement for a lush, tropical isle—the sparkling emerald-blue water, the nearly white sand and the palms—except for the foul smell emanating from the partially decomposed body of a woman half submerged in the water washing up on the beach.

The day had been one of birth and demise, a day of suffering with joy as its climax and with terror and death at its end. It was a typical day in the war. I looked at the body bobbing face down in the occasional swells. No one would search that rotting corpse.

"What a stink," someone gagged.

"Isn't it all?" I answered.

Chapter 11

An Uncommonly Fine Soldier

To this day I am able to vividly recall Private First Class Lewis Albanese primarily because of his face. It was what you would call cherubic, with an impish smile affixed thereto nearly all the time. The first sergeant would remember him because he was, well, perhaps just a bit scattered when it came to things military. The time he presented himself to me for guard duty, but had forgotten to bring along his weapon, is a case in point. A great kid, but just your average soldier, I thought. He was to prove me wrong.

On December 1, 1966, PFC Albanese was serving in Bravo Company's Second Platoon when it was ordered to move to the aid of C Troop, 1st Battalion 9th Cavalry, which had one of its platoons under heavy fire and pinned down in the hamlet of Phu Huu, located in the Kim Son Valley.

The choppers, which would normally have flown in a quick reaction force to relieve the beleaguered men, were grounded by poor weather. Second platoon of Bravo was the nearest unit available. Bill Kail's men were ordered to move north as rapidly as possible, and attained the hamlet area without incident in about an hour and a half. "We near 'bout run the whole damn way," recalled one trooper.

As the lieutenant attempted to make contact with the 1/9 Cav unit, his men deployed with Staff Sergeant George Porod's squad on the left, flanked by Staff Sergeant Jeffrey B. Neher's squad on his right. Specialist Fourth Class Carter Henderson, who had lugged his M-60 machine gun and an M-72 Light Antitank Weapon (LAW) the entire distance, set up the gun to provide cover for Neher's squad, which was preparing to advance on a small group of hooches on the fringe of the village. Unfortunately, protective cover was at a premium, and when an AK-47 fired from a concealed bunker located inside one of the huts, the squads were caught with very little to hide behind.

Actually, they were in the Vietnamese equivalent of a graveyard. Henderson was set up on the top of a grave and was firing over the heads of his squad at the bunker, but was unable to neutralize it. Armed with two LAWs, Jeff Neher was within twenty-five meters of the bunker.

Carter Henderson with his M-60 machine gun

However, in spite of repeated attempts, both weapons failed to activate. Still under fire whenever Henderson couldn't keep the NVA's head down, Jeff called for one more LAW. Henderson, whose gun was drawing more than its share of enemy attention, had the only LAW available and heroically crawled to his sergeant. Just as he passed the weapon to Jeff, a single round struck the machine gunner in the chest, mortally wounding him.

Sergeant Neher, on his third effort, scored a near-miss with the LAW, but failed to destroy the bunker. Bill Kail, frustrated at the performance of the LAWs, ordered his squads to fire and maneuver in an attempt to knock out the enemy position.

Lewis Albanese was in Porod's squad. The sergeant was a giant man with a red face and deep blue eyes overhung with bushy, red eyebrows. He was renowned for the most luxuriant, red, very nonregulation handlebar mustache. If he had been dressed in skins, a helmet with horns on it, and armed with a shield and spear, you would have mistaken him for the original Viking warrior.

Sergeant Porod's men began to move on the hut and its bunker. Almost immediately, PFC Clifford Garska was wounded in the chest and the arm, but, after bitter fighting, the bunker was neutralized. The platoon, still under sporadic fire, continued advancing through some dense brush which seemed to separate the main village from the huts on its fringe.

As they emerged from the heavy cover, Porod noticed what he thought to be a drainage ditch about ten meters to the squad's left. Almost simultaneously the ditch became the deadly leg of an inverted "L" and the platoon was enfiladed by automatic and individual weapons fire. They had been sucked into the killing zone of an "L" shaped ambush.

Neher and Porod were confronted with a number of bunkers and connecting trenches. Both squads were in mortal danger and fought desperately to overcome the well-fortified enemy. Although no one realized it at the time, they were eventually able to do so because of Lewis Albanese, who happened to be on the extreme left of Porod's squad. Apparently realizing that his sergeant and the remainder of the men were in serious trouble, Albanese entered the ditch and moved, with bayonet fixed, down its length, assaulting the NVA fighting positions.

Meanwhile, the two squads came under some particularly effective enemy fire from a bunker located along the ditch. Porod assaulted the position, but was beaten off with two of his men wounded. When he and Jeff Neher mounted a second attack, they found the enemy gunner already dead from small arms and grenade fragments. They also found Lewis Albanese. Official Division sources describe him as being "found dead in the ditch at the head of a trail of eight NVA bodies which he had killed before being killed himself." He was completely out of ammunition, had no more grenades; his bayonet was bloody. The bunker he had just silenced yielded one light machine gun and six assault rifles.

Captured documents indicated the battle was fought against the 18th North Vietnamese Army Regiment. After eleven hours of close combat, some in the pitch dark with the foes just six feet apart, the North Vietnamese broke contact and fled. Sixty-seven enemy bodies were counted at first light. Four wounded enemy were taken prisoner and a host of weapons seized. Bravo Company suffered six killed and eleven wounded. Those totals could have been much higher except for Lewis Albanese's actions. Without regard for himself, he was credited with single-handedly breaking the back of the heavily fortified ambush. How many lives he saved by his actions is speculation. However, there is no doubt he very significantly influenced the battle.

The battalion commander asked me to write up an award citation for Albanese and I went out to interview Bill Kail.

"What do you recommend, Bill?" I asked.

He looked at me as if the answer was too obvious to warrant a reply.

SSG George Porod (left), Ralph Cryer (center) and Medic Erwin Wood with two NVA captives taken at the battle of Phu Huu

"Bernie, he saved our butts out there. All alone. No covering fire. Eight or nine NVA regulars he confronted face to face." He hesitated; his voice had taken on an uncharacteristic emotional tone. "He deserves nothing short of the CMH."

Everyone agreed at every level of command, and for his actions, Lewis Albanese, an uncommonly fine American soldier, was posthumously awarded America's highest award for valor, the Medal of Honor.

Chapter 12

Ung Nguyen's Gamble

"That piece of reed sticking out of the top up there don't look right, Sir."

Several of us were standing near the bunker when one of the men from the Third Platoon made that observation. Most Vietnamese houses had bunkers in which the occupants could find some protection from artillery and bullets. This one was built above the ground due to the elevated water table in that area, and was impressive because of its size—mammoth, about eight feet high, twelve feet long and as wide at the base as it was high, giving the impression of a giant, overturned whaleboat with the keel somewhat flattened. The structure was covered with packed dirt, except for the very top where loose sand had been spread, and protruding from that sand, straight up, was the piece of brown reed about three inches tall.

Except for its size, the bunker was unremarkable and non-threatening. That being the case, several of us scrambled to the top. Once up, we were immediately aware the reed was hollow and almost certainly not there by chance. The sand obviously had been firmed by someone's fingers to secure the reed in place. With that discovery I began to feel uneasy. Could be we were standing atop the biggest booby trap in the war. Without awaiting formal orders, some of the troops cautiously backed off the bunker, while one started to gingerly excavate the loose sand about three feet away from the reed. Not far below the surface he struck wood, then enlarged the excavation until he had completely uncovered what appeared to be a coffin. Bored through the lid of the box, just about at the point where you would expect the head of the corpse to be, was a round hole into which ran the hollow reed; as we knelt there, curiously staring at the lid, the reed moved. Something, or someone, was buried alive in that box.

We understood his name to be Nguyen—pronounced "new when"—the same as our interpreter. Our Nguyen happened not to be with the company at the time, forcing us to rely on Captain Hitti's Vietnamese which was far from fluent.

"Ung Nguyen," the man kept repeating, as he bowed stiffly from the waist to anyone who resembled an authority figure, particularly the captain. Unfortunately, he would always append some other words to the sentence in the choppy cadence typical of the Vietnamese language, which made his monologue quite unintelligible to us.

"Ung Nguyen," he said at last, pointing to himself without appending anything additional. "Dai Uy," pointing to the captain. We knew that dai uy, pronounced "die we", was captain in their language. We finally had Mister Nguyen identified for certain.

Ung Nguyen did not have the appearance of a typical rural Vietnamese. I guessed his age to be about fifty, but physically he appeared less worn from hard work than the average. Many peasants were pitched forward slightly at the waist, no doubt the result of carrying heavy loads or from bending almost double to plant and harvest rice. Nguyen stood rather erect. His grey-streaked hair had been cut by a practiced barber, not hacked at by his wife or some would-be coiffeur. He was somewhat portly and looked a bit soft, not sinewy and hard muscled as were most rice farmers and fishermen of the region.

He was dressed differently also, in white loose-fitting pants and a white shirt worn out at the waist, as opposed to the black pajamas outfit favored by most country Viets. His garments appeared to be a better quality. The typical farmer's calico noir looked to be a very rough, coarse material; Nguyen's was a much better grade of cotton. We had observed that most peasants were barefooted or wore footwear akin to shower clogs, while this man had leather sandals.

The Vietnamese peasant bowed to us in a kind of cowering manner, as a supplicant. He clearly held himself in a lower social position, no doubt from fear rather than conviction. He would bow very low, exaggeratedly so, at times more than once in rapid succession. His hands were usually clasped at the stomach, eyes lowered, but darting upward occasionally with a worried look. I had the impression Ung Nguyen didn't initiate bows, but responded to those of others. He held his arms straight down at his sides, in a relaxed fashion, and bowed slowly, as one in his culture bows to an equal. He was clearly a man of stature in that small portion of Vietnamese society that was his universe.

The building in which he lived was atypical also. Most rural Vietnamese reside in a three-room affair, sided with woven bamboo plastered with mud, and roofed with a reed or rice thatch. Ung Nguyen's home was constructed of block plastered with a smooth stucco finish and white-washed. Beautiful mandarin-orange colored terra cotta tiles served as roofing. A wooden door and slatted window shutters were entirely out of keeping with the surrounding structures, which were no more than the usual hooches to be found in a rural fishing village on the South China Sea.

Far more unusual was the fact that Ung Nguyen was there, standing before us, at all. Typically, we would pass through village after village where only older women, young children and very old adults were present—few young women, no males under the age of sixty at all. The reason for that phenomenon is the nature of guerilla warfare.

A soldier has a grudging respect for the other uniformed man shooting at him. The fellow is only doing his job, trying to survive, just like you. He probably joined his army to put some rice on the table, or was conscripted, and ended up fighting Americans a long way from home. The guerilla is another breed altogether. He smiles at you one minute and kills you when your guard is down. You don't really know where he is lurking. He or she is indistinguishable in the general civilian population, just another person in the crowd. He kills or maims, and then melts away. Therefore, to the soldier, the civilian often becomes synonymous with the enemy. As a consequence, all civilians were treated with suspicion or worse, and many were hauled away for questioning as Viet Cong suspects.

We Americans didn't give much thought to traveling far from home, but most Vietnamese peasants had never been more than a few miles from their birthplace and didn't wish to be. Their entire existence revolved around the family and their village. The thought of being treated as an enemy suspect, or taken into the army, both of which meant long journeys away from the family and home, was not welcomed. Therefore, anyone of military age, or anyone who might be thought of as a guerilla, fled before the troops reached their hamlet.

Yet, very unexpectedly, when we entered his hamlet, there was Ung Nguyen awaiting us.

"This guy must have guts," one of our men suggested in an admiring tone.

No question about that.

The afternoon was well along before we had been able to work our way into his village. Third Platoon led the advance, contending with a single pesky sniper occasionally plinking at us as we approached the scattering of huts shaded by palms. Finally, that weapon went silent just prior to the platoon entering Ung Nguyen's village.

The man must have understood what was coming toward him. He must have imagined how angry the soldiers would be after a day of being targets, particularly since some of the shooting came from his own hamlet. He could only expect, at best, to be considered a VC suspect and hauled off for interrogation. Yet, he was there. He didn't flee as did all the others; he couldn't. You see, Ung Nguyen was the head of a family, a man with heavy responsibilities.

We hadn't ever seen a Vietnamese family, not really. We saw only the old folks and the children. We didn't see the fathers playing with the kids, parents taking the family on an outing—all those domestic activities we take for granted. For all the weeks we had been in-country thus far, we had only seen pieces of Vietnamese life.

In retrospect, I'm not certain we wanted to see the human side of the Vietnamese peasant. Lumping them into the "enemy" category helped to turn off any empathy. They were easier to deal with that way. We were much more cautious of them if they were thought of as the enemy; now, unexpectedly, we faced this man, in every good sense of that word.

A woman in her fifties, presumedly his wife, appeared inside the door of the house. A look of concern was apparent on her face as she stood with just her head visible around the door jamb, the remainder of her body unseen, as if she were shielding it from the soldiers' view. A plain, wooden coffin was positioned outside the front door. Just a rectangular box, nothing fancy, austere by our standards, but, I suspect, the best that part of Vietnam could offer.

Soon after we cleared up the question of Ung Nguyen's identity, a commotion ensued as one of our men tried to enter the house to conduct a search. Second Platoon had been ordered to carefully check all the buildings in the village. The woman didn't want him to come in and had gathered up enough courage to make that known. She started to jabber something while gesturing emphatically and unmistakably, in spite of the language barrier, for our man to get out of her house. But a word from Ung Nguyen silenced her and the trooper entered and looked through the rooms with the woman right behind him. He emerged a few moments later.

"There's an old geezer in the back room, Captain. Looks to me like he's near dead."

John and I entered Ung Nguyen's home, which was furnished more completely and comfortably than anything we'd seen, or ever would see, in the Vietnam boonies. Inside one back room of the house was an old, old man, perhaps Ung Nguyen's father, in a coma, on his deathbed. No doubt the pine box was for him. We were beginning to understand why Ung Nguyen didn't leave.

John Hitti stood rather respectfully before the old man. He asked the medic to check the wizened body drawn up on its side in a fetal position on a wooden plank bed, cushioned only by a reed mat. The old fellow, with skin drawn tightly over his bones, was not much more than a skeleton. He lay there dressed only in brown boxer shorts. I had the thought he must be cold, and looked around the sparsely furnished room for a blanket, but there was none to be seen—just bare plastered walls and a single table and chair. Doc confirmed that the ancient was alive, but seemed beyond knowing. We all quietly exited the room and the house.

Ung Nguyen was visibly more relaxed now. Our troops were dirty and grim after a physically and emotionally exhausting day, but he must have realized that these men were not undisciplined. These troops were under control. However, he no doubt noted, with a concern unnoticed by us, that the soldiers continued their search of the village.

To that point Ung Nguyen's huge bunker hadn't received much attention from the search parties, since a good deal of activity by the command group was taking place just in front. No one had yet taken notice of the lone reed. However, Ung Nguyen's mind must have been working overtime with the thought that the bunker might be thoroughly searched at any moment—because he had more than one secret hidden in its recesses. Consequently, the father took a chance; he gambled. From behind a false wall at the darkened rear of the bunker, he brought out of concealment two young women I took to be his daughters. I was not surprised he had chosen to hide the girls. Any father would have done the same under those circumstances, for obvious reasons. Both were young women, in their late teens or very early twenties, extremely attractive. Their demeanor left little doubt they were very frightened. If our men had been unruly, Ung Nguyen probably would have kept his daughters in hiding and prayed they weren't discovered. However, because there was yet another secret connected with the bunker, he no doubt thought the more prudent course was to be honest with the Dai Uy, as far as he could, rather than risk having the girls discovered by the soldiers. He probably hoped that his being so apparently forthcoming would convince the Americans that no one else was in the village; and, in fact, the platoon leaders soon reported that the huts and their surroundings were empty. Only Ung Nguyen and his family remained in the village.

Shortly thereafter we noticed the reed atop the bunker.

The lid of the buried coffin was not nailed down. With weapons at the ready, we opened the top and pulled from the box a struggling young man in his late teens. He was physically fit, dressed only in green boxer shorts. He could easily have been a Viet Cong guerilla, yet he didn't have the look; he wasn't acting like a guerilla, either—not defiant. Instead, he was frightened and stood with his head bowed, glancing furtively at Ung Nguyen who was, from his facial resemblance and similar hair cut, more than likely his father.

Ung Nguyen seemed frantic and was speaking in an imploring tone to Captain Hitti, undoubtedly pleading that the boy was no guerilla and that no harm should befall him. Night was fast approaching, however, and John didn't have time for a discussion. The young man was bound and led off to the First Platoon area, where he would be kept under guard for the night. The father was escorted to the house and made to understand he wasn't to emerge until morning. The last thing I recall seeing that night was the mother standing in the door, a worried look on her face, watching her son being led away. John Hitti was caught between a rock and a hard place. His face revealed the dilemma. Ung Nguyen had not been totally forthcoming. To that point we had been impressed with this guy. He deserved respect for holding his ground in a very difficult situation. However, hiding the boy cast the situation in a different light. The son might have been the stay-behind sniper who delayed our advance, perhaps allowing his comrades time to escape. After they were gone, he had just to hop into the box and have his parents cover him up. We couldn't tell. In any case, he would have to be considered a prime VC suspect, a source of information that might save lives. The regulations were clear about suspects; John had to turn him over to the Division Intelligence people who would, in turn, hand him to the South Viets. There was also the numbers game to take into account. The brass in the rear were always pressing for body count, prisoners, captured weapons and the like. The boy's capture couldn't hurt John's record.

Ung Nguyen had gambled. He had not fled. In doing that, he ran the risk of being taken away if the Dai Uy thought he was Viet Cong. He brought his daughters from hiding with the hope that the soldiers would search no further and to show his good faith. But he dared not risk his son, who Ung Nguyen undoubtedly believed would have been impressed into the army or executed as a guerilla if he were caught. Now the captain could only assume he was VC. The government would be informed that Ung Nguyen had a son who had been hidden. He would be considered a guerilla. The family would now be suspected guerilla sympathizers. Ung Nguyen had gambled to keep his family together. He had lost. Things would now get very much worse.

The old grandfather passed away about four in the morning. We knew because the women started to wail a lament in the house. With the daylight, Ung Nguyen looked a tired, broken man. No doubt he was awake most of the night, even prior to the old man's death. He and his wife carried the coffin into the house. Both returned to the door as the troops were departing, and I guess they expected to see their son hauled off with us. But John Hitti brought the boy to him, untied the young man and motioned that he could stay there with them. Then he shook hands with an awe-struck Ung Nguyen, bowed as a man does who respects another in that culture, and turned to depart the village. Ung Nguyen summoned his composure and returned the captain's bow with a quiet word I took for a thank you. A tear was rolling down his wife's cheek. The daughters were nowhere to be seen.

I never asked John for his rationale for doing what he did. I didn't really have to. John Hitti was an extraordinary person, an excellent soldier and a man capable of great compassion and deep feeling. He recognized and respected bravery, and he understood why Ung Nguyen acted as he did; he was a father himself. As we left the village, I caught John's eye and gave him a smiling thumbs-up sign. He smiled back and went on without a word.

The day was beautiful. Bright sun had replaced the previous day's rain and a sea breeze would moderate the afternoon heat. The sky over Vietnam was an unpolluted, intense blue. Up ahead, Third Platoon started receiving sniper fire. Another battle, another day of gambling the ultimate was beginning for us. Ung Nguyen had won his.

Chapter 13

The Enchantress

The village was little more than a widening of the paddy dike which created an island of sorts amid a sea of bright green, ripening rice. There were perhaps eight or nine typical Vietnamese huts. We found the dwellings deserted except for one old man and a young woman who were sitting on the ground outside a hut. The old fellow looked every bit the typical farmer, with sun-darkened, weathered skin, and dressed in tattered black shorts and a grey shirt. The young woman, on the other hand, was extraordinary for a number of reasons. Her skin tone was very much lighter than the man's and her facial features were more caucasoid. She sat stripped to the waist with her legs drawn up under her, wearing a kind of brown sarong. A suckling baby was cradled in her arm. She had an attractive face, not worn; her black hair was loose and fell to shoulder length. Her breasts hung full as might be expected with a nursing mother, large but not overly so. I was struck with the thought that she looked just like an enchantress—an absolutely beautiful, totally unexpected, incongruous sight. We were field troops, not Saigon warriors; Vietnamese farm women did not look like this.

"Circe."

A voice brought me out of my reverie.

"What'd you say?"

"Circe, the temptress. She delighted in attracting men to a cruel fate. Mythology, Sir; Greek mythology."

The soldier schooling me on the ancients was a bookish looking kid whose name I'm unable to recall. Although he had the youthful appearance of one who should still be in high school, he was supposed to have completed two years of study at some cerebral New England college, got bored, and decided to see the world by joining the Army. I'm not sure what he was smoking when that idea was hatched.

"If I had to guess what Circe would look like, at least from the neck down, there she is right there."

The old man was chattering at us. Although we could not comprehend him, there was little question from his facial expressions and posturing that he was angry. He continually motioned for us to leave, occasionally shaking his fist. The woman was just sitting and rocking, almost as if she were in a trance. The thought struck me that she was a little out of her mind. In retrospect, I know she was— with fear.

The two Vietnamese were seated on the bare ground in front of a hooch, about twenty feet inside a fence. That enclosure surrounded the hut, a water buffalo stall, and a hog pen. A couple of lazy porkers lay in the pen, but there were no buffalo to be seen. The fence was strongly built, of sticks dug into the ground to form a tight irregular barrier about four feet tall, interwoven with brush. I could see through the interwoven material, but it would be difficult to penetrate. We were standing in front of the only break in the obstacle, a six feet wide opening, closed off by a gate. Gates were, however, an easy way to get killed.

Several of the men moved closer to the fence. The woman was really an extraordinarily beautiful sight. Their approach caused the old fellow to shout louder at them. He was jabbering nonstop now and gesturing for us to get the hell out of there. The woman started to get more excited also. She seemed to be rocking back and forth more quickly.

At first I believed the old man was just trying to protect his daughter from the approach of these gawking soldiers. But if that were the case, why would she be sitting there to begin with, instead of out of sight in the hut? Circe sat in all her glory with only a piece of loose cloth covering her below the waist, almost as if she were inviting trouble. Her eyes were closed as she rocked back and forth. I thought the look on her face, however, was that of barely concealed terror, utter fright to the point that she appeared to be deranged. Neither she nor the old man moved from their spots, as if they were anchored down. Perhaps they had been ordered to stay there. It was a safe bet that no woman as attractive as she would willingly remain, sans clothing, in front of strange soldiers. Never had we seen a Vietnamese woman this naked. Even mothers who were forced by necessity to nurse a child in our presence did so with far more modesty.

A strange, mental tug of war was going on in my mind between the desire for this lovely vision to be just what she was—a beautiful woman nursing a baby, nothing more than a pleasant contrast to war—and the more obvious thought that the situation was so bizarre it required investigation. Once I opted for investigating, caution returned. The man and the temptress were now the enemy.

Wanting to investigate is one thing; doing so was quite another. Our common practice was never to go through a gate; they were often booby trapped. Even the fence could be mined. The people could be booby trapped, for that matter. Why else would they be sitting there in the hot sun? Perhaps there were Viet Cong in the hut, waiting for us to make a search as was our practice. They could take us apart while our return fire might be blocked by the woman and the old man. Perhaps the woman's husband was hiding in the hut, trying to avoid us. Maybe that's why the woman was outside and not out of sight inside. A number of possibilities ran through my mind very quickly, including where I could dive for cover should the worst happen. The situation certainly looked like a trap, with the woman as bait.

Just about then a stream of tobacco juice and saliva landed a few feet in front of my dusty boots. Sergeant Truman Humrock usually announced his arrival in that manner. He was a mountain man from West Virginia and the only person in the outfit who could stomach chewing that glop. A man of few words, the Sergeant quickly distilled the situation down to its bare essentials.

"Ah don't like it, Sir. Looks like a set up."

"Circe," our pedagogue cut into the conversation as though he were far away, lecturing in a classroom. "She turned men into animals, the animals they most nearly resembled—usually a jackass."

A jackass was just about what I felt like at that moment. There was nothing obviously threatening to be seen, but, with the exception of the old guy jabbering, our surroundings were very still and quiet, unnaturally so.

"Sure as hell doesn't look good, Sarge," I said, almost in a whisper, with my mind reverting from investigating to just plain getting the heck out of there. "I believe that old man wants us to leave and avoid trouble for everybody. Where are the rest of the men?"

"Well, Sir," he drawled, "havin' a pinch more horse sense than some I know, they're coverin' your asses from the ditch behind us instead of standin' in the open gawkin' at a pair of tits."

"Thank you for that bit of wisdom, Sergeant. If you and the others will back off easy, I'll cover you while we disengage here."

As the two troopers backed off, I looked again at Circe. Was she a trap? We never knew, because prudence dictated we leave. Always better to avoid the bait than struggle in the snare. No sense in getting into a fight with civilians in between. Whatever victory, if any, came of the violence that might ensue just didn't seem worth the possibility of destroying those three people, all that beauty.

Chapter 14

They Finally Got Walt Swain

The soldier was lying on a standard, olive-drab litter used by the medical people, supported off the floor by two fold-up metal frames that looked like saw horses. The canvass was much too short for the lanky frame. Over the end his bare feet hung limply, turned inward toward each other. One deeply sunburned arm had fallen off the table and dangled toward the dirt floor. The other rested awkwardly across his chest. He was clothed only in well worn fatigue pants blotched with reddish brown patches I knew were dried blood. Thrown on the floor amid a half dozen or so bloody field bandages was the soldier's fatigue shirt, its green color turned almost completely red-brown. The nearly obliterated name tag read "Swain". His eyes were closed as if he were asleep and his face appeared to be at rest, calm, without pain. There were no marks on his body, no wounds except for his head which was covered in a mass of white bandage.

"Walt," I whispered, bending to bring my face close to his left ear.

I felt out of place. Actually, I'd been kicked out of that very tent more than once. The doctors didn't permit any non-medical types in their treatment area. Often times I'd slip in to give a wounded man a word of encouragement and end up getting ejected for my trouble. I felt like an intruder who shouldn't be there, a feeling that compelled me to speak in the hushed tones which seemed appropriate to the moment.

"Walt, are you awake; can you hear me?" I tried again, this time nudging his shoulder.

There was no hint of a response. He felt cold despite the suffocating afternoon heat. I stared intently at his naked chest, stark white in contrast to his sun burned arm, trying to determine if he were alive. I could see the rib cage rise and fall almost imperceptibly, irregularly I thought, with his shallow breathing. For some reason the dangling arm troubled me and I repositioned its dead weight across his chest. He looked more comfortable that way.

I looked around. The heavy, olive drab tent was completely closed up, allowing almost no outside light or fresh air to enter. The smell was a heavy mix of hot canvass and antiseptic. Along the tent's periphery, in deep shadow, were chests filled with the tools of the medical profession. Suspended in the center, over the litter, was a large light, its illumination directed straight down in a powerful beam. Hanging from hooks above were bottles of clear fluid turned upside-down, with plastic tubes dangling toward the body. The place looked like an operating theater prepared for the surgeon's knife. But it was empty, except for the two of us, and abnormally hushed and quiet. The usual external noises of a combat evacuation hospital seemed to have diminished drastically, so much so that I could hear him pull in a ragged, labored breath.

Looking at him in that helpless condition, I couldn't help but recall his former self. Walt was the kind of guy nearly everyone wants to look like, handsome to a fault, tall, blond hair, blue eyes, thin and muscular. If you needed to cast a green beret officer for Hollywood, Walt was your man. To compliment those physical attributes, he possessed an impish grin and an engaging personality. In his dress uniform he cut a classic military figure, career Army, doubtless on the way up in rank.

Momentarily, I was filled with a surge of anger. Where the hell was everyone? Somebody ought to be working on this man, keeping him alive. The emotion passed quickly, however, replaced with sadness as my brain accepted the grim reality that the medics had done all they could. They would be here otherwise, wouldn't have given up and left him. This was the essence of triage. Those whose prospects of surviving their wounds were nil or nearly so were set aside until the more lightly wounded received attention. I knew the doctors were in the next tent working on a trooper who had been brought in with Walt. That man's chances were better. I looked again at the bottles of fluids. Although filled, they weren't connected to the body. I understood then that Walt Swain was nearly brain dead. The world was simply waiting for the remainder of his being to give up the struggle.

War Story is a book written by Jim Morris—his Vietnam autobiography. To me the most memorable words in that work were, "So they got Walt Swain." The words in context were a predestined fait accompli, as though Morris knew there was only a matter of time before Captain Walt Swain would be killed. Walt, himself, didn't think he'd ever get home again. According to Morris' account, he told his wife, Hildegard, that he wouldn't; and she spent from August of 1966 until April 26, 1967 waiting for the Army staff car to arrive at her front door with a dour-faced chaplain who would break the news.

Jim Morris and Walt Swain had served together during their first tours in RVN, in the good old days, if any could be called that, when Kennedy's iron men were holding strategic posts in the more remote parts of the country. Walt and this guy had swashbuckled through a year's bloody tour, outnumbered by the North Vietnamese, often outgunned, always on the verge of disaster.

Morris learned of Walt Swain's fate on the tarmac of an

airfield outside Kontum City, in the western central high-lands. He had approached a group of 5/7 Cav troopers, looking for Walt. They told him that Captain Swain was dead. The troopers didn't know exactly how he died; they were from another company, didn't know the details.

"It came through that the bastards had finally got Walt Swain," was the cryptic epitaph.

What Morris was unaware of then, and when he wrote his book, was exactly who "the bastards" were. Who were "they" who got Walt Swain?

Walt served as Battalion Intelligence Officer (S-2) through the first half of our tour in Vietnam. His driving ambition, however, was to secure a company command. He felt he needed that on his records.

"Nothing better in the personnel file than a combat command," he once said to me.

He was given Delta Company early in 1967 and there was no question in anyone's mind he really loved the assignment. I had a hand in preparing the personal letter the battalion commander wrote to Hildegard after Walt died. He/I told her that her husband was the happiest man in the Cav and we really believed that.

Walt Swain was a particularly good and effective small unit commander. He could motivate men to give 110% all the time, and he did so by personal example. On March 7, Delta Company discovered a cave thought to be occupied by Viet Cong. Our troops yelled and screamed into the murky interior, trying to get anybody inside to come out, but their efforts yielded nothing. The simple answer to the situation was to just heave an explosive charge into the hole and bury anybody inside, but Walt wanted them alive for their intelligence value. (Once an S-2, always an S-2.) He particularly wanted any weapons that might be in there with them, knowing that if there were any, the Viet Cong would dig them out as soon as the Americans were gone. Telling his men to stand back, Walt stripped off all his gear and, armed with only a pistol and a grenade, he approached the

*Battalion Intelligence Officer, later Delta Company Commander,
Captain Walt Swain*

cave, pulled the pin on the grenade and gently placed the
thing right at the entrance. The grenade went off with a
blast which quickly convinced six guerrillas inside to sur-
render. I suppose they assumed the next one would be
tossed in with them. All six exited unarmed which posed
a dilemma, that being—were there weapons in the cave and,
more nerve-wracking, were there any more bad guys in
there with them? Having had plenty of cave crawling experiences during his first tour, Walt didn't ask one of his
men to run the risk and go in, but went in himself, armed
only with his pistol and a flashlight. He emerged shortly
with a big smile and five rifles.

Some would consider that good leadership, some fool-
hardy. Whatever you term it, that was quintessential Walt
Swain.

On April 26, an assault was to be made by Company C
on a suspected enemy village in the An Lao Valley. The
action was to be supported by tanks, that being one of the

few portions of our operations area accessible to armor. Walt Swain and Delta Company took up blocking positions along a road leading away from the target village, and were soon rounding up a steady stream of enemy suspects being flushed out by Charlie's sweep. Sometime later, the tanks started to reposition themselves in order to better cover our men.

At 1253 hours the Tactical Operations Center at Battalion received an urgent request for a Medevac. The notations on the radio log read: "1253. D Co to TOC—Require MED EVAC for 2 persons—one is D Co CO he was hit in head—not sure if it is a short artillery round or a round from a tank."

At 1315 Walt Swain was brought by chopper directly from the field to the 15th Med at LZ English, and placed in the tent where I found him.

I filed the required casualty report concerning Walt later that day in An Khe, and received a call from Major Bullock. He and Walt were close friends. Both had agreed that if either of them were killed or wounded, the other would make certain the deceased's personal effects were returned directly to his wife. At the time, however, the Major was unable to fulfill his end of the pact. He explained his predicament and asked me to help. During that same conversation, he told me he was going to find out exactly what happened to Walt, because Delta Company hadn't been in close hostile contact at the time he was hit.

Except for some personal pictures of his wife and two pretty little girls, everything included in Walt's gear at An Khe was government issue which I sent through channels. Several days later, I gave the pictures to the Major for him to mail. He showed me a copy of his inquiry into Walt's death.

Tom Bullock was a man for detail. Particularly in this case that trait served him well, because he was determined to find out how Walt died. His report impressed me with its thoroughness. He went out into the area where Walt was hit, and reviewed the entire sequence of events with those who were there, including the tank crews. He plotted exact locations of the armored vehicles, Delta Company, and Walt. He measured distances and angles. The Major concluded that Walt was struck with a shell fragment as he sat in the open, watching some of our armor engage a distant target.

Captain Swain's position, indeed his entire company, was not receiving any incoming fire from the enemy. There was apparently no danger at hand. The day was very warm. Walt was in an open area with no shade and had removed his steel pot to get a break from the heat. He was sighting through his binoculars.

The tanks were not firing in any proximity to Walt. However, one of the rounds from a main gun apparently struck a solid object, causing a piece of the shell to ricochet, drastically altering its initial trajectory. That fragment then impacted a tree close to Walt and the flight was considerably altered once again. After glancing off the tree, a fragment struck Walt. Pieces of it also cut down the other trooper injured in the mishap.

The "they" who finally got Walt Swain in Jim Morris' book weren't "the bastards" at all. "They" were us. Walt Swain was another victim of friendly fire. "They" were him and all who knew their promotions would be greatly enhanced by a combat command. "They" were all our presidents and politicians—the ones who never got on the tiger's back—who sent nearly three million men to Vietnam, but lacked in themselves the political will, intelligence and nerve to make the decisions necessary to win.

Chapter 15

The Bronze Age
And The Machine Gun

In the Central Highlands one could stand atop nearly any prominence and observe a sea of yellow-green grass stretching for hundreds of square miles, broken occasionally by patches of heavy forest, brush and trees. Beyond the grasslands rose the mountains. The French referred to the war they fought in that same area as "la guerre des grands vides"—the war of the vast empty spaces. These seemingly limitless areas were sparsely inhabited by the Bahnar and the Hre tribesmen—Montagnards, the Mountain People.

The dark brown Montagnards were locked in the Bronze Age, almost literally. They were hunter-gatherers, semi-nomadic people who manufactured nearly everything they used—pottery, baskets, clothing. In warm weather the men wore little but a loin cloth. The women fashioned a sarong from the black and red material they wove, and often went bare breasted. They possessed a few metal utensils, just knives and axes, and for hunting used cross bows.

Montagnards fought with the U.S. Special Forces because they hated the North Vietnamese who would impress them into service to fight a war, the politics of which they knew nothing about and cared for less. Other groups of Montagnards fought against the Saigon government because the ethnic Vietnamese treated them as second class citizens, at best.

The government's solution to the problem of Montagnards fighting with the NVA and Viet Cong was to resettle as many as possible out of their remote, mountain homes into camps closer to population centers; there they were under the "protective" guns of the ARVN. Once the camps were established, other Montagnards migrated there to avoid having to fight for the North Vietnamese. Unfortunately, these new homes were far from the haunts of the game the mountain people used for food. To a great extent they became dependent on the government's largess.

One such camp was located outside An Khe, quite far off the highway, out of sight. The dwellings were a collection of huts on stilts, much smaller shelters built on the ground and old military tents. An obviously new well was in evidence. The huts looked new also, but were roofed with corrugated tin and probably bake-oven hot, inasmuch as the camp was built in the tall grasses with no trees to dissipate the sun's heat. We were cautioned by our ARVN interpreter not to enter the living areas. The men will "not much like you do," he explained. However, there were no male adults to be seen, just a gaggle of smiling children dressed in torn or very well used western dress. I did glance in one of the smaller huts and glimpsed a young woman sitting in the dust near a fire pit. She was nursing a baby boy while a young girl observed and learned her future. I was struck with the paucity of their possessions—a few bowls, one clay water bottle, a large basket and a few pieces of cloth.

Returning to An Khe we chanced to meet two Montagnard men on the way. They were coming back from an unsuccessful hunt. The younger carried a cross bow and

Montagnard man with his cross bow, outside An Khe resettlement camp

Montagnard mother with all her worldly possessions in
resettlement camp outside An Khe

was pulling on an empty clay pipe. The older carried nothing. Both wore loin cloths. I didn't use cigarettes, but always had a pack or two to give to the Vietnamese. American tobacco was much in demand and cigarettes represented a good way to start a conversation. The pipe smoker didn't light up the cigarette, but carefully pulled the gift apart and filled his pipe. I offered him a light, the remainder of the pack and the matches. He seemed very appreciative. We conversed through the ARVN representative and I asked why they moved to the camp, curious to know if they had been coerced. Both looked at the ARVN with impassive faces and, without a word, turned and left.

Several weeks later, I was sitting beneath a leafy canopy overhanging a shallow creek. Savaged by a brutal sun, we had walked for hours that morning through the high grass of those grands vides and we welcomed the moderated temperature the shade provided. With the sunlight dappling through the trees, the scene was nearly idyllic. I established a security perimeter and we quietly broke out some C-rations for a noon break. Just then I noticed the first signs of human habitation I had seen that day.

On the ground about ten feet from the creek were a number of narrow, clay vases about three feet tall, very reminiscent of Roman amphora. They were uniformly brownish-black in color and were all partially buried in dried mud that must have come with the rising water of the rainy season. Some had tipped over and were nearly covered; some were still upright, encased in earth part way up their sides. Unquestionably, they had been there many years. Some were more ornate than others, with carrying handles and with designs etched into their sides. One or two were strikingly worthy of being collected, so fine was the workmanship. They were all empty.

What were these vessels?, I wondered. Was their purpose for carrying water from this stream, or for storing food? There was little question they were highly prized utensils, but why then were they left out here so far from any village, a place without any sign of past habitation? Could the village from where they came have survived their loss? Undoubtedly, some disaster struck those who carried them to this place. Perhaps they were taken captive during the First Indochina War by a patrol much like my own. There was little doubt in my mind the vases were Montagnard in origin.

In that quiet, beautiful glade with the sun filtering through the trees and the stream making slight, splashing noises as it ran over rocks, the war was far away. The setting was exactly opposite to what we had already seen or heard of the conflict and I wished my world could remain that way, but knew better. Looking again at the artifacts, I found it impossible not to liken those voiceless, mysterious sentinels with Keats' Grecian Urn—his ". . . foster child of Silence and slow Time . . . Sylvan historian, who canst express . . . What legend haunts about thy shape."

What could these mute historians tell us of their owners who failed to return? They couldn't say, and we left them as they were found, witnesses to a tragedy many years prior.

I understood for certain then what caused the Montagnard men to live at the resettlement camp. No doubt they were forced, just as the bearers of these silent sentries were forced to abandon their precious cargo, by one warring side or the other, when the Bronze Age met the machine gun.

Chapter 16

Better Than Just OK

I first noticed Specialist Fourth Class Tony Tabaso at the end of a long training day; he was crossing the battalion parade ground at Fort Carson with a gaggle of other bone-tired troopers. He stood out because, in addition to his combat pack, canteens, pistol and the other normal paraphernalia, he was hauling an M-60 machine gun, a tripod and two ammunition boxes. That's more than a full load for any man—his assistant gunner was nowhere to be seen—and, more remarkably given the late hour, he was concomitantly whistling a happy tune.

The men I was observing were machine gunners from all the companies in the battalion and were, at that moment, under the direction of a sergeant first class. I walked over to him, intent on commenting favorably about the troop with the heavy load.

That day, perhaps because I was a relatively new boy on the block, having just been assigned to the battalion, he was clearly unimpressed with my observations.

"He's OK, I guess," was the extent of his comment.

Everyone is entitled to his own opinion, but my perception was that any soldier who enjoyed humping an M-60 machine gun day after day was a great deal better than just OK—masochistic perhaps, a bit crazy maybe, but not just OK.

My feelings for machine gunners were born of my own brief experience with the weapon in Ranger School—two full days in the steep North Georgia mountains—from which I gained a first hand appreciation of what it took to carry that weapon, and I was hauling it sans the ammo boxes and tripod. No, in my book a good machine gunner rated more than just an OK.

That summer, 1966, will be remembered not only as the time of the 5/7Cav's departure for combat in Vietnam, but also the summer of the airline pilots' strike, an action which shut down nearly all commercial air travel in the country. As luck would have it, the start of their job action coincided with the return of the battalion from our predeployment leave. Many of our men were stranded or faced the prospect of a long train ride and a late arrival, even if scarce rail reservations could be obtained. I found myself negotiating with a harassed Air Force sergeant in an effort to get manifested on anything moving west out of McGuire AFB in New Jersey, when a voice from behind asked, "Say, Captain Grady, can you give us a hand gettin' outta here?"

It was SP/4 Tabaso, his ever present smile betrayed by a worried look in his eyes.

"We've been bumped I don't know how many times," he continued, "by anybody with three stripes or better."

"We?" I asked. He was alone.

"Yes, Sir. There's a bunch of five-seven guys here; and, Captain, if we don't make it soon, my first sergeant's gonna be pis . . . ah . . . aggravated—yea, that's it—he's gonna be aggravated if I don't get back on time."

"Knowing the first sergeant, Tabaso," I said with a grin, "your initial thought was probably more appropriate."

There were literally hundreds and hundreds of service personnel at McGuire awaiting transport to every part of the globe. Tabaso and I finally rounded up nearly a full squad of 5/7 Cav troopers from among the mass of bodies.

Combat orders gave us a priority, but even with that it took thirty-six hours before my makeshift squad could get off. On the flight, I took the opportunity to get to know Tony and to pump him for everything he knew about the M-60. He'd packed that weight all over Fort Carson and declared himself and his gun ready for combat.

By the following morning, our flight had deposited us at a remote, Colorado Air National Guard base. I cannot imagine why they unloaded us there. I suppose someone drew a straight line from McGuire to Travis AFB in California and this forgotten airfield fell on the line.

"How do I get these men to Colorado Springs?" I asked the Flight Operations Sergeant.

"No problem, Sir," he answered. "We were alerted that you'd be along and we've laid on a National Guard flight to get you home. He's up now circlin' the field, burnin' off fuel so's he can get over the mountains."

I was becoming impressed with Air Force efficiency, and didn't ask if the aircraft was of the Wright Brothers vintage or a later model. However, the question was soon answered when an aging, twin engine DC-3 landed.

"Your winged chariot has arrived," the sergeant announced with a mischievous grin, as the propellers came to a stop with a wheezing, popping, whistling finality.

I noticed Tabaso's face slowly registering the horrified realization that this relic was to be our transport.

"Captain Grady, I'll take the bus if you don't mind," he said, looking around for an escape route.

"Tabaso, they resupply this place by mule train. We're already a day late. Now how do you think the Top is going to feel when we report in a couple of hours from now and I tell him you'll be along sometime next week?"

"Aggravated," was his dejected reply.

The flight, although a white knuckler for our brave machine gunner when we hit some turbulence, was in keeping with the unparalleled safety record of that aircraft, and we were soon back at Fort Carson.

In the next few hectic weeks before departing, I didn't

see much of Tabaso and, because in Vietnam we operated most of the time as separate companies, I didn't get to see him in action until a few days after I assumed command of Charlie Company.

We had air assaulted into a quiet landing zone atop one of those extremely narrow ridge lines that characterize the mountains in Binh Dinh Province; we were to be picked up that afternoon on the same terrain feature a dozen kilometers to the north. The mission was a simple search and destroy.

This wasn't the best place in the world to maneuver four platoons. The ridge fell off steeply on both sides, effectively forcing the company into a long column, with my units advancing along a narrow front perhaps forty meters wide. Down slope movement would be difficult and in some places impossible.

Very early in the march, the ridge line pitched downhill for about two hundred meters of intermittent, waist-high grass, and then uphill again for an equal distance to a heavy forest covering the next peak. Beetle Bailey could have figured out that if any unfriendlies were occupying that wood line, my boys would be deep in more than grass if just a single heavy weapon hit them halfway to the other side. My forward platoon leader had spread his men out as best he could on the very narrow spine and, with more than a few misgivings, had started down the slope when I called him back.

"Lieutenant, your ass is grass if any Charlies are over there," I said, motioning to the other side of the dip.

"I thought about that, Captain," he responded with a look on his face and a shrug of his shoulders which indicated to me that he knew he was going against the odds, but wasn't certain what else to do.

"Ammo's cheap, men aren't," were my initial words to him. Then I took him aside and followed up with some unprintable expletives and a few more restrained words to the effect that I expected he'd bring more grey matter to bear in the future. This was my first command, let alone a combat command, and I really wouldn't want the Old Man to have to bail us out of a mess.

"I want you to set up your machine guns and do a recon by fire on that woods and anything else that looks like a hiding place for VC. As soon as your last man clears this point, the next platoon's guns will pick up where you left off. Mortars," I yelled, "set up your tube and be prepared to put rounds right on the peak of that ridge. I want to be able to adjust from that point into the wood line if we have trouble. Questions?" There were none.

Seldom have I seen men happier to do a job. "Ammo's cheap, men aren't" represented the defining moment when I, as the new commander, put my personal stamp on Charlie Company. It declared exactly how I planned to operate and exactly how I felt about the safety of my troops.

I was having the mortar platoon get their tube laid in case we needed them, when Tony Tabaso and his gun came forward.

"Tabaso."

"Sir," he answered coming closer with a smile and look on his face which led me to believe he knew exactly what I was about to ask.

"Know what I mean by a recon by fire?" I knew he did; we'd talked about it on the white knuckle flight.

"On the wood line?" he answered.

"You got it, hot shot. I want a base of fire to flush any VC over there, and while you're at it get me a good fix on the range for the mortars. That'll save us wasting any 81 rounds."

"Ready, Tabaso?"

The platoon started forward.

"Yes, Sir."

"At your command, Tabaso."

I watched him smile as he aimed and silently mouthed, "fire".

Click—nothing happened. He went into his malfunction drill, quickly reaimed and squeezed the trigger. Two rounds sped toward the wood line before the gun jammed, permanently.

"Lieutenant, get me another gun. Tabaso, clean that weapon."

Four more guns malfunctioned before we got an M-60 to put out more than three consecutive rounds. It was obvious those weapons hadn't seen any use for some time. To say the least, there were more than a few embarrassed faces around and none more red than Tony Tabaso's.

There weren't any enemy in the woods, and after we had gotten through the day, I called the platoon leaders and sergeants together to emphasize the point that they were responsible for seeing to it that those guns worked. Failure to do that meant to me that they didn't give a hoot about their men.

"There WILL be no more guns that don't fire," I said.

Tabaso came by later to quietly pledge that his gun would never malfunction again. Fate would test his resolve.

"Routine insertion, quiet LZ, no enemy known to be in the area." That was the intelligence report the Division G-2 conjured up out of his crystal ball.

The quiet landing zone was anything but, and I found myself behind a paddy dike facing a bunch of AKs positioned in fighting bunkers at the edge of a village.

My primary concern at the time was for those of my men who were pinned down and possibly wounded. An assault on the enemy force had to be accomplished fast, but to do that I needed some additional riflemen. Fortunately, the company hadn't been too badly scattered and John Long, excellent executive officer that he was, advised he had some warm bodies coming quickly. Our mortar and M-60s went to work. Shortly, a squad came crawling through the muck. Pulling up the rear of that small relief party was Tabaso, carefully, and with great effort given its weight, cradling his M-60 clear of the filthy water. Behind him came his assistant, equally as carefully holding two boxes of 7.62 ammo out of the wet.

"Need some help, Captain?" Tabaso asked, flashing a your-problem-is-ended smile.

"That gun gonna work, friend?"

"You can bet your bottom on it," he countered.

"I'm about to do just that, Tony. That's why I asked." The smile disappeared.

I positioned the M-60 on my extreme right flank with the idea he'd provide covering fire during our assault. I was getting some effective use of my other guns, but I knew I'd have to call off those weapons almost as soon as the assault got going. Therefore, Tabaso's M-60 was going to be critical.

The buck sergeant who led one of the fire teams took up a position to the right of his men and next to Tabaso; I was in the center of the assault line with my radio men; further to the left was the other fire team with their squad sergeant. That was my army just then—about fifteen men and a machine gun.

"Tabaso, open up!" I yelled, saw him swing the gun up on the dike, and almost immediately heard the first rounds. He was right on target.

"Assault," I yelled and my troops were up and moving with what I thought was a very disciplined volume of fire as we advanced.

Assaulting a hostile position is an experience I don't recommend. There is no place to hide; you're in the open and, once started, there is no turning back. An infantry assault is an all-or-nothing proposition, and it is the place where you most appreciate good covering fire to keep the bad guys' heads down. Tabaso was giving us just that. It wasn't possible to move quickly in the muck and it seemed to be taking forever to reach the objective. I was very cognizant of the M-60. Tony was doing it just right, controlling his fire and reaiming after each burst. Then, with the assault line only a quarter of the way across the paddy, the gun fell silent.

My practice has been never to speak badly about any of the men under my command. Each man has his limitations and, in my experience, nearly everybody in combat does his best; but that fire team sergeant was not playing the game with a full deck. His M-16 had jammed and, attempting to clear the malfunction, he wandered to his right, promptly masking Tabaso's gun. Tony couldn't continue to fire for fear of hitting him. What was worse, the sergeant, totally engrossed with the mechanical dilemma, had no idea what he had done.

It is a military axiom never to discontinue an assault, never go to ground in the open. I noticed a slight hesitation in the forward motion of the line when the gun quit, but I urged the men on, shouting, "Keep going—don't stop—control your fire—go, go, go." My efforts, however, were totally outdone by the squad leader on my left whose booming voice produced a rather more colorful monologue. We still had a long way to go, or at least it seemed so. Then, unexpectedly, the M-60 blew another burst of six into the bunker line, and another. I glanced to my right and saw that somehow Tabaso and his assistant had sprinted in front of the wandering sergeant. Tony was firing the weapon from the hip as we closed, looking for all the world like an early-day Rambo, with his AG still feeding rounds from an ammo box as they moved.

There is nothing like the heavy, thudding sound of an M-60 to bolster one's determination. "Let the bastards have it, Tony," I yelled and then screamed out my version of a war whoop which was immediately repeated by nearly every man in the assault line.

It was all over quickly and we were mopping up when Tabaso asked, "How'd we do, Sir?" He was speaking of himself and the gun.

"OK," were the first words from my mouth, but I caught myself and quickly added with a smile while slapping his back, "Better than that, Tony; damn good, damn good."

"Told you never to worry about this gun again," he said with unconcealed pride and a grin to match.

He was right. I never did.

Chapter 17

Brutality

Each time I saw him, the poor fellow appeared to be bleeding from another part of his face. At first I disregarded his condition. In a war, debris and pieces of metal do tend to fly about. Perhaps he had been cut that way prior to our capturing him. However, a short time later the man was bleeding from two fresh places.

"He fell down, Sir," came the remark by one PFC, a member of the squad charged with guarding him.

I hadn't posed the question before that answer was volunteered. A genius was not necessary to fathom that something was amiss.

"Well, gents, if this man falls again," I said, emphasizing the word falls, "or if his body shows any more wear and tear than I presently see, I'm gonna have somebody's ass. This guy might have some useful intelligence information in his head. When we get things stabilized here, we'll get him to an interpreter, but in the meantime I'll be damned if that head is gonna end up looking like it got the worst of a brawl at the club."

We had been fighting for control of that gent's village and I had directed some artillery rounds into the area from which the hostile fire had come. However, when we entered the hamlet, we found no enemy bodies that could be identified as such. The lack of verifiable enemy bodies was not an unusual situation in that war, but it was frustrating for the men who had just witnessed one of their friends killed. A single enemy KIA would have given them some feeling of parity. Even so, there was no excuse for the breakdown of discipline, never a justification for mistreating a prisoner.

When we entered, the hamlet was empty except for the lone, Vietnamese male who stood before me bleeding, but with the same smile on his face that was present when we first encountered him. He was typically dressed in a pair of boxer shorts and nothing else, and he sported the worst haircut I've ever seen. His coiffure looked to be the result of his mother putting a very shallow bowl on his head and chopping away at anything it didn't cover, but botching the job at that. There was little question this was not your normal Vietnamese farmer. First, he was unique for that smile. Normally, people didn't smile when captured by mean-looking guys wearing mud and watery grime from having been prone in rice fields. The smile itself was odd, in that the fellow's lower jaw jutted off to the right, his lips looked forcibly drawn apart, and his teeth were mashed tightly together. Then he stumbled forward a bit and I realized he balanced on the outside edge of his right foot, almost over on the ankle. His right arm was bent at the elbow, up tight against his chest, with the wrist hanging limply toward the ground and fingers cramped back toward the palm. Obviously, he was the victim of cerebral palsy or something similar; that, or he was a very good actor, which didn't seem probable under the circumstances.

The battlefield situation at that moment was "fluid", a military term which meant I wasn't certain what the heck was happening. Several huts were on fire from artillery. The dry thatch used for roofing material was burning fiercely, igniting the bamboo siding of the huts. The bamboo burned with intermittent loud pops and cracks, sounding much like a rifle being discharged. Each time that happened, everyone ducked reflexively. In addition, there were several louder explosions from the burning buildings, indicating that ammunition or explosives had been concealed in the thatch. Everyone was somewhat on edge. My immediate concern was for the tactical situation. Accordingly, I had left the captive with the squad that found him hiding in a hut, while I tended to more pressing matters.

It was incredible to me that these men, (men or man, I wasn't certain who was doing the damage, not having seen a blow struck), American soldiers who up to that point had been models of proper military discipline as far as I was concerned, would be beating on this obviously handicapped fellow. For a brief moment I had even entertained the notion that perhaps he actually did stumble and fall; God knows, the man had difficulty just walking. However, when I finally did get the company in order and returned to the man, he was much the worse for wear. Now, he looked as if he was definitely hurting; even the smile was gone. I suspected from his posture, now rather bent over at the waist, that someone might have hit him in the stomach.

I had a quick choice to make. The company had been ordered by the battalion commander to reestablish contact with the enemy. We had to advance immediately and press forward rapidly. With no time to call for a chopper to evacuate him, I would be forced to take the captive with us in the belief that he could provide useful intelligence information; or I could simply let the fellow go free and spare him some grief and pain.

The Army frowns on anyone who knowingly allows a piece of potential intelligence to slip away. I could find my own butt in a sling if anyone got wind of my setting this guy loose. Just because he had a physical handicap didn't mean he was an imbecile or couldn't communicate. On the other hand, he was certain to slow us up and would probably "fall" more than once between here and the end of the day. Additionally, the poor guy was certain to face some South Vietnamese interrogator, a none too pleasant prospect.

I set the captive free, a decision from the soul, not from the hard-bitten, win-at-any-cost book of military doctrine. Whatever information he had, if any, was not worth the physical and psychological pain he'd have to endure. Initially, he didn't comprehend that he was free. I had to physically turn him in a direction away from us and give him a gentle push. He looked puzzled, then thankfully giving a few quick bows, he disappeared into a hut and we didn't see him again.

I thought my men looked more or less relieved, at least most of them. One or two looked angry, probably those precipitating the captive's "falls". No one in the squad guarding the man would admit to harming the prisoner, nor did anyone see his buddy perpetrate the deed. Since I couldn't identify the culprit, I let the first sergeant know of my dilemma; I noted soon thereafter that the squad in question was pulling more than its share of fatigue duties, particularly the dreaded latrine cleaning detail, whenever we got back to a place where there were latrines.

That was the only case of outright brutality I witnessed among the men I directly commanded. Another case of criminal brutality I observed was committed by a South Vietnamese soldier assigned to another company in our battalion. Private Trung, as we shall call him, was a good soldier. He was in his early twenties, intelligent and, previous to this event, had not been given to bursts of rage.

Charlie Company had conducted a search operation through an area of moderately heavy forest. The company to which Trung was assigned had been placed in a blocking position to our front. We apprehended several young men along the way who were clad only in undershorts. They would turn out to be North Vietnamese regulars. These gents, as was so often the case, decided to conceal their weapons and uniforms and try to pass themselves off as farmers. They were healthy looking men, very physically fit and disciplined; there was no way they would pass for the sinewy, bent-backed planter and harvester of rice.

Another characteristic which gave them away was their deportment. Normally, the peasant would assume a fawning attitude when confronted by troops, acting friendly and bowing repeatedly. In marked contrast, these guys scowled and stood with heads bowed, refusing to look you in the eye. Trung questioned the prisoners and declared them to be NVA. At least they were speaking a North Vietnamese dialect, had no identification and couldn't name the local villages or village chiefs.

The plan was for Charlie Company to spend the night in the field. The other company would return by Chinook to LZ English with the captives. While we waited for the big transports to arrive, Trung continued to talk to the prisoners. One of them seemed to be in charge and wouldn't allow the others to speak. The two were conversing in Vietnamese, but obviously an argument was in progress. I noted that Trung decided to walk away from the discussion. Unfortunately, the NVA honcho said something clearly very uncomplimentary as a closing riposte; it was his final remark. Trung, his face showing uncharacteristic rage, grabbed his M-16 by the barrel and swung at the man, full force. The NVA soldier was half sitting against a tree stump, hands secured behind his back, with what appeared to be a satisfied grin on his face. The lower butt piece of the M-16 struck him full in the left temple with a sickening crack. The man dropped like a stone.

Trung's astonished commanding officer quickly subdued him with an angry reprimand. The ARVN never said a word, but his face had a plaintive look on it, not so much in sorrow for the damage he had done, but more for himself, that he had succumbed to the taunt. Shortly thereafter the choppers arrived and two of the departing company each grabbed a foot of the unconscious man and ran through the prop blast to the chopper which was some hundred feet away across a plowed field with deep furrows. The NVA soldier was like a rag doll, arms outstretched, completely limp, mouth open, his head bouncing rapidly from furrow to furrow. They dragged him up the rear ramp of the chopper, his head striking its metallic edge, and threw him into the cavity of the ship as the ramp closed.

The other company commander said he would handle the affair. I don't know if he did, or if so, how. Being an ARVN soldier, Trung's misdeed would have come under the military codes of his country. I doubt that his superiors would have pressed the matter, inasmuch as he was an exemplary soldier, but I do not know that for certain.

Although I cannot vouch for all the other American soldiers in our battalion, these two incidents were the lone cases of outright prisoner mistreatment I witnessed. Additionally, I was unaware of charges brought against any of our men for such conduct, and, as the S-1 for a time, I was in a position to know.

There were probably others, unreported. Abject cruelty, as opposed to a loss of temper, requires only opportunity, no motive. There was plenty of opportunity. We were at war.

Chapter 18

Death In A Very Dark Place

I was perched on my upturned helmet—an attempt to keep my butt out of the water running down the hill—soaked with rain cold enough to produce a recurrent shiver the length of my body. My poncho was draped over me to the forest floor. The hood of the clammy, waterproof material covered my head so that only my face was exposed to the rain; it had fallen, first as a heavy shower and then as a constant drizzle, since late afternoon. As I leaned against a large tree for support, the heels of my boots dug into the hill, helping to maintain a precarious balance on the curved helmet and preventing me from sliding down the slick slope.

The night was intensely dark. The rain clouds and the nearly complete forest canopy conspired to prohibit what light there may have been in the heavens from reaching the hundred or so men scattered about me. Everything was uniformly black. For all intents and purposes, we were blind.

The darkness was so complete that only sounds existed, and in the rain there were more of those than we wanted. The drops escaping from the leafy canopy landed on the forest floor with a plop, blotting out the more subtle noises of the night—the movements of small animals in the humus—sounds which are normal and nonhostile, the absence of which may mean danger is at hand. Unable to hear properly with my head covered by the poncho hood, I hooked the material behind my ears and moved my head from side to side like an imperfect radar, trying to pick out any unusual noises.

Satisfied that all was reasonably well, in so far as I could determine, I pulled my head down out of the hood into the small area created by the fabric as it draped off my shoulders and over my knees. In that cavity my face, cold from the night air and the rainy mist, immediately sensed the contrast between the outside and what warmth existed in my body. The only hint of light was the green glow of my watch face which read 2100 hours. A soft hissing sound, not audible outside, came from the vicinity of my left leg. I flicked on my flashlight. A red filter over the bulb to preserve night vision turned the cavity a dim scarlet, and illuminated the M-16 resting across my lap and the two radio handsets hanging across my left thigh. The hissing sound emanated from the handsets. The radios were outside, covered with plastic to protect them from the wet. Both were leaning against the tree with their ten foot, whip antennas extended, providing the connection between my company and the battalion, and me with my four platoons crouched in the night around me.

I squeezed the soft, rubber transmit button on the handset monitoring the company net. The hissing stopped.

I whispered into the mouthpiece, "One-Six, this is Six, Sit Rep, Over," then released the button and listened intently. Almost immediately the hissing was broken to silence, came back on, and then was broken again, as the radio operator from my first platoon signaled his situation report. Two breaks of the hissing meant all was well. I repeated the process with the other three units, getting identical responses.

The company was in what could only be described as a precarious position. Hastened by the low clouds that brought the rain, darkness overtook us before an adequate defensive perimeter could be established. I was very uncomfortable with the situation.

Earlier that afternoon the Old Man ordered me to air assault Charlie Company into a wild, mountainous area in an attempt to exploit a "hot spot". The Intelligence folks at Division, using infrared photo imagery, had located an area beneath a very heavy forest canopy which was showing "hot" relative to the surrounding terrain, thus indicating the possible presence of enemy personnel or cooking fires. Division wanted a quick look into the area that day. Bold Eagle got the job.

To avoid putting us into a hostile landing zone or the possibility of spooking the enemy, the air assault inserted the company on the top of a ridge line about two thousand meters from the target. We went in without benefit of any artillery prep. The time was approximately 1500 hours, late for the mission because of the approaching darkness. With platoons in column, I moved Charlie quickly along the ridge. When we reached a point that was above the target, the two lead platoons turned right and started down the steep mountainside, with the third platoon trailing in reserve and the mortar set up in the grass to provide support.

Within thirty meters of the crest of the ridge, the platoons plunged into forest which had at least a double canopy, the tallest of the trees being perhaps one hundred or more feet in height. Beneath those giants was a tangle of lower trees, brush and vines sufficiently dense so that entire squads disappeared into them. The command group, located just behind the two lead platoons, had no sooner entered the heavy brush when a single discharge from an M-16 was heard. Thinking that someone had accidentally fired his weapon, First Sergeant Westmoreland took off to chastise the offender (as only he could), but returned quickly to report that one of our men had engaged a uniformed Vietnamese and wounded him. Unfortunately, the man was able to flee along a path that led down the hill. Since enemy soldiers in uniform didn't wander around alone, we had every reason to believe there were more of them down slope. Accordingly, we proceeded carefully, in retrospect too slowly, down the mountain through the heavy brush, with the forest canopy growing more dense as we went. About one hundred meters further down, we came to a deep ravine with nearly perpendicular walls along its fifty meter length. At the bottom a series of caves could be glimpsed in the sides of the ravine, perhaps twenty in all, no doubt man made. Several cooking fires still smoldered, but there were no enemy in sight. Probably the guy we shot earlier was an up-slope lookout. Obviously, he had spread the alarm. The question in my mind was—where did he and his buddies go and how many were there?

Fortunately, despite the light rain, flying conditions were not below minimums; in response to my earlier radio message that we had engaged the enemy lookout, the battalion commander was overhead in his charlie-charlie. True to his nature, which dictated that he always support his men with maximum firepower, the Old Man brought along a gun ship which spotted, through an opening in the trees, something strange on the forest floor about two hundred meters to the left of our general position. War Paint Six ordered us to check it out.

Lieutenant Rick Belt's First Platoon was on the left flank, and I gave him that mission while I consolidated my forces. Clearly, we were on the spore of what could have been a reasonably large enemy unit, probably main force Viet Cong or North Vietnamese regulars, judging by the lookout's uniform. With Rick soon to be some two hundred meters to our left, my company was effectively split into four separate units. Third Platoon was down slope and chomping at the bit to get into the caves and see what the quickly retreating enemy might have left us. The mortar men were still back up on the ridge, and Lieutenant Doug McCrary with Second Platoon was physically separated from the main body of the company by the ravine itself. My concern was that, if we came under attack, the platoons could get chewed up piecemeal. I ordered the mortar to join us and set up a perimeter facing up the slope. Once in the trees, the 81 tube was of no value, but with night falling I needed the rifles of the platoon in an infantry mode. I told Doug to hold his position and prepare to defend our right flank; Three-Six was ordered to dig in, defending down slope with an M-60 and some Claymores positioned to fire on anyone trying to get in or out of the cave area.

Rick Belt excitedly reported finding field packs, large sacks of rice and bloody clothing. I asked him to bring them back to our position.

"Eagle Six, One Six," he responded over the horn, "no can do. Must be a hundred of them, plus the rice!"

We had, indeed, come on a large unit. The fact that they were uniformed and with field packs definitely ruled out any notion they were a local, ragtag guerrilla outfit.

From the War Paint Charlie-Charlie, an obviously elated commander chimed in that a net and sling would be dispatched to our location. Two choppers arrived surprisingly fast and, with some expert flying skills, managed to get the nets down to Rick's men who made short work of loading out the material they'd found.

"These guys are gonna be mad," Rick announced over the radio.

"How's that?" I asked.

"Wouldn't you be if some guy just walked off with your last pair of skivvies and socks?"

By the time Rick completed his job, the radio transmissions from the Old Man had a worried tone which matched my own feelings. A company-size, enemy unit was out there somewhere, and they knew well the ground on which we were operating. The colonel wanted us to start moving toward an open area they could see on the valley floor, perhaps five hundred meters away. I told them it was too late. It may have been twilight up there, but below the canopy someone had turned out all the lights.

I tied Rick in with Four-Six and Three-Six, but there

was no time to coordinate defenses or to dig fox holes. We were crouched nearly shoulder to shoulder in makeshift fighting positions, but anyone ten feet away wouldn't have sensed our presence. There was scarcely a sound. Every man understood that at least a company of enemy troops might be close at hand, perhaps maneuvering to attack us. Even if they did nothing more than return in an effort to get their packs and try to shelter from the rain in the caves, there might be hell to pay.

The watch read 2130; I was getting drowsy and needed to poke my head outside into the cold and jar myself awake. Inside the dimly lighted cavity, I actually felt warm for the first time in hours, and as obscure and temporary as the red light seemed to be, at that moment it represented what was good and normal with the world. There was something comforting about being able to see, about being just a little bit warm. Outside, the dark and the cold symbolized the chaos and evil that was the war. I didn't want to go back out into the dark terror that was the night, back to the cat and mouse game where death was the loser's reward. For a long moment, there was the nearly overwhelming temptation to close my eyes in the warm and go to sleep, but I couldn't yield to the temptation. I did, however, allow myself a glimpse at civilization, a letter from Christine which I hadn't had time to read carefully. Normally, I destroyed my mail before going into the bush. I didn't want to risk being captured bearing a letter that the enemy might use to my detriment. I read the note over several times. Mail was often difficult. The words were too much a reminder of home and what we were all missing and risking. I carefully tore it into tiny pieces which I mashed into the wet earth. The onion skin absorbed the brown moisture from the forest floor and smudged the blue ink. In the red light, the color of what remained of the paper mimicked congealed blood. Civilization was gone; its demise brought me back to the task at hand. I flicked off the flashlight and poked my head up through the hood of the poncho into the wet cold.

There was no change in the night except that the rain had diminished, leaving us with a steady drip of moisture off the leaf tips, and an occasional downpour when a strong gust of wind shook the tree tops. Blowing from the east, the wind in my face was off the distant sea and had an awakening effect. Mixed with it was the odor of humus from the forest floor—a familiar smell to an infantryman, not unpleasant, and necessary in such a pervasive, black void where the mind demanded something more tangible than just the sound of the drips to keep the senses oriented. There was nothing to be seen or heard in the darkness, so I ducked back under the poncho.

The silence was broken by a call from Two-Six advising that his men were reporting sounds, possibly moaning, coming from the depths of the crevasse. Three-Six confirmed the sounds and thought there might also be some movement out to their front, but they weren't certain. At that point I ordered a full alert and had our supporting artillery fire at a point straight down the hill about five hundred meters away from us.

The initial shell impacted in the valley to our front. With two more rounds, I moved the impact toward us to a spot where I could actually observe the flash of the shells as they detonated down the hill. To give my men a little confidence and to ease any case of the jitters they might have been developing in the dark, I worked over the hillside with the entire artillery battery. If the noises that Third Platoon thought they heard were, in fact, the enemy, I had just brought down a dozen rounds of high explosive on his head or very close to it.

To me there was something very elemental about artillery. A few words over the radio, some calculations, several adjustments to inert pieces of metal, activate the firing mechanism and enough force to destroy a human being or an entire building is racing towards its mark. The men on the receiving end hear nothing of the gun's discharge, only the uneven sound of the shell arriving, like a jet plane striving for the sound barrier, until the round impacts, first with a crack and then a blasting sound. The World War I poet, Wilfred Owen, described exploding artillery as, ". . . the hot blast and fury of hell's upsurge." In Vietnam I came to view it as cold death from above. Using artillery brought an almost mesmerizing sense of raw power and destructive potential. Artillery allowed one to kill at a distance, kill impersonally, and kill without ever knowing the victim or, indeed, if there was a victim at all. A large shell can destroy a body beyond recognition, reduce it to vapor. Artillery is man's inhumanity to man without the guilt. Only the grief remains, somewhere.

Author (center) with weapon of captured NVA soldier (right)

In the midst of all this activity I received a call from the S-2, advising that the unfriendlies in the ravine were thought to be a Main Force, Viet Cong battalion aide station or something akin thereto. Documents in the enemy packs had been translated at Division and the aide station conclusion seemed to fit the bill. The number of packs and the variety of documents indicated that the VC medics were caring for more than a few wounded when we interrupted them. Obviously, the news that we had chased off a medical unit sat a good deal better than had it been an infantry company. Chances are those medics were carrying more medical supplies than weapons and ammo, making an attack by them somewhat remote. Three-Six was no longer reporting any movement to his front, so I called off the full alert and the remainder of the night passed uneventfully. The noise from the crevasse had ceased also.

A search of the caves next morning produced several weapons, more bags of rice, and a single Vietnamese male. He had been wounded sometime prior to our arrival. His injuries were too extensive for him to be moved with the others. He was dead when we found him. No doubt the noises in the night were the last sounds the man made. For a brief moment I felt sorry for him. By himself in the pitch dark of the cave, death must have been terrifying and lonely. My compassion did not persist. As usual, I had too much to do and think about to insure our own survival.

We were fortunate that night. Death in that very dark place had visited someone else.

Chapter 19

Tobacco Man From Somewhere

The dike served as a road of sorts, albeit a narrow one fit only for small carts and foot traffic, across a stretch of mangrove swamp—an old dike judging from the scrub trees and brush which covered the steeply sloping sides. The top was bare. Perhaps for a millennium, countless traversing feet had packed the surface cement hard, had worn away what grass and vegetation may have attempted to put down roots on its flattened crown. Standing atop the dike, you were perhaps five feet above the level of the fetid, ominous looking water below.

"Where's this miserable dike go to, Sir?" The question came from the Point Man crouched behind some sparse cover, eyes intent on the tree line to his front.

"Nowhere—at least nowhere that I can tell. It's not on here as a road or anything," was my reply, as I intently studied my map, trying to fix our position.

"Has to go somewhere, Captain. We left Nowhere this mornin', goin' to someplace that Charlie don't want us to get to. Why else would he be shootin' at us all day?" The Point Man had a mischievous grin on his face, pleased with his contorted logic.

SNAP.....Crack.

As if to emphasize his point, the VC fired at us again. The noise on the receiving end of a bullet shot from long-range is a vicious snap resembling an electric current arcing from conductor to conductor, not the bang you hear on the trigger pulling end. The snap is followed in a second or so, depending on the distance of the weapon to your ear, by a crack, as the sound of the discharge, traveling slower than the bullet itself, catches up. Sometimes that following sound is a bang, depending on the type of weapon being fired. That day the Viet Cong seemed to be shooting small bore weapons at us—they cracked.

"See what I'm talkin' about? That VC don't want us to go to Somewhere. And this gent coming towards us, now he's on his way from Somewhere going to Nowhere, and you can bet your rosy red ass he's really going nowhere if he makes the wrong move." The Point Man sighted down his rifle toward an indistinct figure slowly moving up the dike.

SNAP.....Crack.

The dike ran from one unnamed group of thatched huts to another equally unsung village—from Somewhere to Nowhere if you bought the Point Man's logic—neither important enough to be on my map. But we had spent a good part of the day trying to span the distance between the two. We were pushing east, toward the South China Sea, pushing the VC back to the water. Theoretically, their escape to the north and to the south was cut off. I couldn't comprehend why they continued to engage us. Nearly everyone else apparently had found a way out of our trap but these snipers. Obviously, they were trying to delay us for some important reason known only to them. At midmorning, however, they must have understood they were in a trap and had to buy time until nightfall, when chances of successfully evading us were greatly improved. About that time they really started to pin us down on the dikes with sniper fire. We'd move a few meters and, SNAP....Crack.

Two hundred or so meters to our front was an island of

sorts in the sea of swamp. The VC had been waiting until we got on the dikes to chew away at us. We could only take cover in the brush on the side of the dike away from the sniper and struggle forward—a risky business; but there was no other way to get the job done. Moving through the water was out of the question.

SNAP...Crack.

We were closer to Charlie now. Earlier in the day, they were shooting from long range and the interval between the snap and the crack was pronounced. We had closed the ground and the two sounds had almost merged. We were nearly accustomed to it. There was still that reflexive duck of the head when the SNAP came, but not as fast as we did at first.

"No sense duckin', man," said the Point Man. "You don't hear the one that hits you."

SNAP, SNAP...Crack, Crack.

"Ain't duckin' from the first one. It's the second I'm getting the hell out of the way of," countered his buddy, hugging the ground as the incoming rounds flew over our heads. "That son-of-a-bitch's gettin' our range."

Suddenly a vicious snapping cut near us again, this time in the other direction, as one of our M-60s positioned some hundred meters to our rear fired a burst at the village. The gunner's job was to suppress the enemy fire so we could advance. Up ahead to the right of the dike, we could see the 7.62 millimeter rounds land low in the water with a series of individual geysers, and then climb forward toward the trees as the gunner adjusted his aim. The heavy rounds hit the trees and brush, occasionally dropping a limb. Every sixth machine gun round is a red tracer, its arcing path clearly visible.

The snipers were invisible. Only occasionally would we see a muzzle flash from the sniper's weapon, attesting to its age. Newer firearms were equipped with a flash suppressor. The age of the weapon indicated we were facing Viet Cong. They had the older rifles; the NVA had AKs.

So our day had gone—crawling forward and ducking—

until the Point Man spotted the figure of a person emerging from the tree line into which the dike disappeared. A Vietnamese man was coming directly toward us along the top of the dike, apparently oblivious to the danger he was courting. He was dressed in the typical black pajama outfit with the pants crawling up high around his ankles and the shirt sleeves too short for his arms. The cloth's original color had faded to a near grey from countless washings and the bleaching effect of the sun. No sandals protected his feet, nor was he wearing the usual coolie hat. From a distance he appeared to be alone.

The Point Man held his fire on first sighting the man far down the dike.

"Crazy son-of-a-bitch must be stupid. Look at him, just as cool as a cucumber."

The Point Man and his buddy held what looked like a very old man in their sights for a long while as he closed the distance between us.

SNAP...Crack.

"Hold your fire," I said hurriedly as the enemy round flew by. "Don't want to waste anybody who looks that old. He's no problem to us."

BANG, BANG, BANG, BANG, BANG—another of our machine guns sent an answering burst. I could see a red tracer round fly by the oncoming man.

"There's somebody hiding behind that guy, Sir. Crazy bastard's gonna get up to us and lob a grenade or somethin' in our laps." There was a tinge of urgency in the voice of the Point Man now.

Clearly, as he got closer, we could glimpse a second set of legs moving behind the first and what looked like two small brown hands gripping the man's hips.

He was an old man, bent dramatically at his waist from years of heavy labor, who could do nothing more than shuffle along the dike. Ho Chi Minh in the flesh—gaunt skin stretched tightly over prominent facial bones, sunken cheeks, with a balding head and a wisp of yellowish goatee falling from his chin. Shuffle-step, shuffle-step, shuffle-step,

each sliding foot moved him stiffly, with barely bent knees
and elbows, another foot or so on his journey towards us,
filling more and more the point man's gun sight. And then
from behind him appeared the face of an ancient mamma
san peeking out to see how much progress they had made
to wherever they were going. Her countenance was a ca-
lamity of wrinkles gouged in every square inch of skin
which, in dramatic contrast to his, hung loosely in folds.
We realized when we saw her that she wasn't deliberately
hiding behind the man, but simply was remarkably short.
She was, in fact, the force propelling him along.

As the situation became clear, I could see the Point Man
relax. The two ancients didn't see him or his buddy as they
shuffled by, but as the old boy got to me, he took notice
that I was crouched there beside the path. He stopped and
looked down. Although the rest of his body looked worn
out and about ready to give up the ghost, his deep-set,
black eyes seemed alive and full of life. A smile crossed his
face, and he opened his mouth revealing a few very yel-
lowed teeth. He pointed inside with a bent finger, and
started speaking at me. At first I had no idea what he
wanted. Even though he could have used some badly, I
didn't think he was asking for dental work. I responded
with a reflexive, questioning look and a negative shake of
my head. He pointed to his mouth again and kept up the
monologue. The old woman, still with her hands on his
hips, was giving him an occasional push, but the old boy
was determined in his quest. I tried to wave him on his
way.

"Di di. Di di." That was the extent of my polite Vietnamese, which can be roughly translated to "please leave."

No dice. He continued to point and jabber.

"Tobacco, he's lookin' for some chewin' tobacco," said
the Point Man who was now laying on his back enjoying
my consternation at not being able to get the old guy going.

SNAP, SNAP, SNAP...Crack, Crack, Crack.

The rounds came in very close, much closer than the
random popping we'd previously experienced, and I real-

ized the old man, standing in the open on top of that dike, obviously talking to someone on the ground, had become the VC's aiming point. They knew he wasn't jawing with some friend of the family out there.

SNAP, SNAP...Crack Crack.

"There's the bastard," yelled the Point Man's buddy as the two of them let loose M-16s on full automatic.

"Di di. Di di," I yelled. More pointing, more jabbering, no movement; but then the old lady realized what was going on and commenced to really push on the old guy as she started to jabber up a blue streak.

BANG, BANG, BANG, BANG, BANG. The machine gun opened up again.

SNAP...Crack. The VC got off another round.

"Di di mau. Di di mau," I screamed at the two old people over the din, at the same time threatening them with my rifle. It was only a matter of time before one of the two of them caught a round in the butt, or one of us bought one, if they didn't get out of there. The addition of "mau", a nasty Vietnamese expletive, the threat with my M-16, and his wife's prodding finally got the man moving. He shuffled off down the dike, much too slowly for my liking. She was behind him, head bent, eyes to the ground, pushing.

We eventually reached the village that day. The Viet Cong were gone. There were just four huts, probably all belonging to one extended family. Three of them hadn't been inhabited for some days. One, however, had seen recent use, probably that very day; the charcoals in the cooking fire were still hot. I never got to look back along the dike for the old couple until much later. They were gone.

I often wondered what possessed them to start out on their journey across the dike. Cynics would suggest they were Viet Cong sympathizers who were sent out to mark our positions. After all, the two of them could have remained in the bunker just outside their hut and have been reasonably safe. They could have also chosen to retreat with the VC toward the sea, across another dike on the far side of the village. Therefore, I don't know why they decided to come in our direction, and I can't bring myself to believe they did so with malice. In retrospect, he was a likable old gent with those lively eyes, and the wrinkled, little old lady pushing him along was equally engaging.

I do hope they were able to return to Somewhere, their home.

Chapter 20

Thanksgiving At A
Secured Landing Zone

Sometime around 0800 hours on Turkey Day, 1966, Charlie Company was ordered to air assault into a not too distant landing zone near where a North Vietnamese battalion was thought to be bivouacked.

"The LZ will be secured by another company." Those were the fateful, last words I would hear from battalion before the operation began.

The first flight of choppers sent to pick us up touched down far from where we expected and refused to come to my waiting men. Further contributing to our growing confusion was the fact that the S-3 Air told me to plan for eight choppers. Instead, we received four on the first sortie and six thereafter.

Third Platoon was designated to be the first unit out, followed by First, Second and Mortars. As it was, First Platoon was closest to the birds and I radioed Lieutenant Rick Belt, ordering him to load on the first four choppers. When the second lift of six birds appeared, the first three picked up the remainder of Rick's men. First Sergeant Westmoreland, three RTOs, a grenadier named Richard W.

"Rick" Smith left over from LT Belt's platoon, an artillery forward observer and I took the fourth bird. The remaining two aircraft carried men from Third Platoon, which was commanded by its Platoon Sergeant.

Although we try to impose some rational order over our lives, we often find ourselves the victims or the benefactors of an uncertain fate. The reassignment of First Platoon to the initial four choppers condemned two men to a death they would probably not have otherwise met.

As my lift approached the supposedly secured landing zone, I was fortunate enough to have a remarkably good, albeit fleeting, view of the surrounding terrain and the tactical situation. The landing area was an enormous, flooded rice paddy separated into individual rice fields by a series of dikes, most of them not much wider than twelve inches and as high out of the water as they were broad. Cutting the paddy in half along its full, north-south length was a much more substantial dike, perhaps six feet wide and three or four high.

HU-IB assault helicopter, with handgrip of
M-60 machine gun in foreground

The forested Cay Giep mountains loomed off to our left rear. At their base was a typical village of twenty or so huts nestled under palm trees. Across the paddy and directly opposite the village was a low hill, no more than fifty feet high, covered with scrub bushes.

To this day I cannot explain what whim or perversity motivated the troops responsible for securing the landing zone. However, as my sortie approached, we could see they were not in the village, but lounging on the large dike and waving at us with big smiles. As we passed, they started walking north on the dike, away from the landing zone. Obviously, they had not done their job. The LZ was not secured.

First Sergeant Westmoreland, who was sitting on the left side of the aircraft, turned to me and shouted over the sound of the rotors and the engine, "What the hell are they doin' there?" There was a look of justifiable concern on his face.

I was unable to ponder the question. My attention was drawn to a spot far across the paddy where Rick Belt and six of his men were slogging through the paddy muck, cautiously approaching the village. When I glimpsed them, they were within thirty feet of their objective.

Staff Sergeant Brent Hodges, one of LT Belt's best squad sergeants, was in the lead because his usual point man, Smith, was on my bird. Edward McElroy was slightly behind him, followed by Bob Wolicki and Leonard Frederick. Rick Belt and his Platoon Sergeant, Paul Riley, followed along at a greater distance with the remainder of Brent's squad.

At nearly the precise second Rick's men came into my view, the NVA took them under rifle and machine gun fire. Brent Hodges was very seriously wounded in the lower abdomen. Edward McElroy, a splendid young trooper, was killed instantly. Frederick was hit in the leg. The remainder went down in the water and foot high rice plants, and tried to slither behind the low dikes so that their bodies were generally protected; but they were unable to return

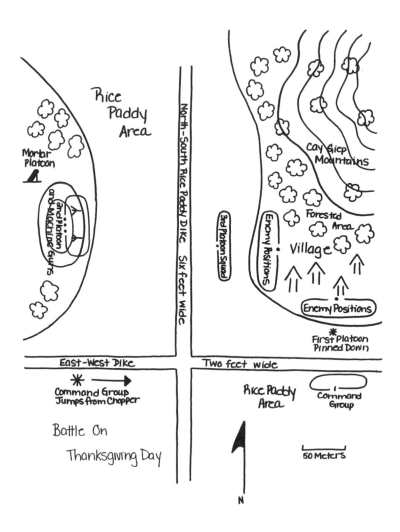

Rice
Paddy
Area

Mortar
Platoon

2nd Platoon
and Machine Guns

North-South Rice Paddy Dike   Six feet wide

3rd Platoon Squad

Enemy Positions

Cay Giep
Mountains

Forested
Area

Village

Enemy Positions

First Platoon
Pinned Down

East-West Dike

Command Group
Jumps from Chopper

Battle On

Thanksgiving Day

Two feet wide

Rice Paddy
Area

1
Command
Group

50 Meters

N

fire. LT Belt said the enemy fire was so close to him that he could see the bullets rip the ripening rice off the tops of the plants. Brent Hodges was so near the enemy, he could hear them talking to each other when there was a lull in the shooting. Having lost his M-16 by the force of the blow to his abdomen, Brent was armed with only a single grenade which he threw at the enemy to help keep their heads down and give him the opportunity to move further away. However, the seriousness of his wound did not permit him to move quickly or very far and he lay, calling for help, almost literally under the muzzles of the enemy guns.

After cutting down the squad, the enemy tracer rounds immediately shifted to the lead two choppers in our group. Those first two aircraft were about six feet off the ground in that semi-stall a helicopter achieves just prior to landing, with their rotor blades creating a hurricane of ripples on the water. The tracers were right on their target and I saw them slam into the aircraft. The pilots' reactions were automatic and instantaneous, causing them to bank radically to the right, and climb frantically. The third pilot delayed just a few seconds and then reacted similarly when he became the next target.

Because my chopper was last in the line of four and some meters behind the others, we had a few additional seconds before the NVA gunner was able to reposition his weapon and sight on us. Our pilot saw the entire event unfolding and no doubt understood that, as the company commander, I would want to be on the ground. Accordingly, he held the chopper in a hover. In those brief seconds I slid to the door and was sitting with my legs hanging out, thinking he'd land. He wouldn't. I turned hurriedly to look at First Sergeant Westmoreland. The Top had also moved to the door on his side and was awaiting my next action. I jumped, followed by all my men.

We fell at least twenty feet into eighteen inches of water and a foot of muck beneath that, which helped cushion a brutal landing. Our aircraft commander was obviously a quick thinking individual, inasmuch as he had taken care to position us behind a dike about three feet high which afforded us protection from the bullets coming from the village.

As I picked myself up, I looked north towards the final two choppers in our sortie, several hundred meters behind. At that very moment all of the men in those aircraft were making like birds also. Their pilots would not land for them either, but did position them about forty meters from the edge of the village, behind a low dike. I was momentarily filled with pride. Those were good soldiers—loyal, tough, knowledgeable and well led. America could have sent none better. My next thought followed quickly and inexorably—"Thank God". If they hadn't jumped, my tactical position would have been very much worse, since they immediately engaged the NVA's flank and gave them someone else to think about.

My group moved east as quickly as the deep muck would permit, duck walking and crawling behind the dike to avoid enemy rounds. Each time I looked toward the village, I could see enemy tracers streaking toward Third Platoon like some malevolent insects gone berserk. Occasionally, those same streaks of green light would flash over our heads or kick into the dike, throwing dirt over us.

I had already made several unsuccessful attempts to talk to Lieutenant Belt on the company net, and assumed his radio was out of order. As we moved along, I put the battalion commander in the picture and asked him to land the rest of Charlie Company behind the small hill from which I planned to develop a base of fire, using my machine guns and the mortar. My intention was to use that fire support to silence the enemy weapons, and assault over the top of the trapped men into the village.

About fifteen minutes were required to reach a point where I thought we were behind Rick's men. I peered over the dike while standing in a crouched position, but the men were nowhere to be seen, having completely submerged themselves in the water behind the dikes. At about that time, Doug McCrary's Second Platoon secured the hill and were ready to crank up the M-60s.

The paddy was shaped like an "L". I had a heavy squad of Third Platoon stretched out north to south on the long side of the "L", while my group was deployed east to west on the short side. Doug's machine guns commenced firing over Third Platoon's heads and into the village. Shortly thereafter, John Long, my XO, reported the mortar was ready to go and, good man that he was, anticipated the need for an ammo resupply and already had it on the way from battalion. I ordered the mortar sergeant to work over the village and attempt to seal off any enemy retreat. By that time, I wanted the guys who were shooting at us, and thought we might have a chance at them if we could keep them out of the hills behind the huts.

Meanwhile, my small force was engaged in a sporadically heavy pitch battle with the enemy. There was one machine gun facing us and three or four other weapons which we thought were AK-47s. Since the NVA were firing from prepared fighting positions, they were giving us hell and then some. The radio operators were quickly out of M-16 rounds. In short order, I had given them all my spare ammo and had to caution them to reserve at least three or four clips. The remainder of the day I was completely out of ammunition except for the single clip in my weapon. While they engaged the enemy, I was working with the artillery forward observer, trying to get some heavy, indirect support.

At one point there was a lull in the fighting and I chose that relative quiet to kneel up on the protective dike in another effort to locate my men. Once up there, I was able to observe some people exiting the village to the east. The first sergeant got up also and I pointed toward the spot. My intention was to alert him to the possibility that, if an enemy soldier was with them, he might work his way around to our right and shoot down the dike, a situation that would have left us with no protective cover at all. I never had a chance to utter a word. The enemy machine

gunner opened fire at us in what apparently was a sweep-
ing motion from his right to left. That was very fortunate.
Had he taken direct aim, I would be history. Instead, as
the RTOs described later, tracers passed behind my back
and then in front of me. Assuming the NVA loaded one
tracer for every six regular rounds, quite a few bullets came
my way. Only one hit, and that was just a glancing scrape
on my right wrist, which I had extended in a pointing
motion. Unfortunately, the gunner continued to sweep his
weapon away from me, catching First Sergeant
Westmoreland in the elbow, a serious injury that would
put the Top out of action in Japan for several months. I
slid over to him, fearing the worst. He looked up at me
with what I thought was a mixture of pain and concern on
his face. That look was so atypical of Sergeant
Westmoreland that I was momentarily given pause. It was
the only time in Vietnam when the thought crossed my
mind that perhaps I was in over my head.

"Hang in there, Top," I said, as I applied his field bandage over the wound which was turning the paddy below
it crimson.

Then just 28 years old, Haskell B. Westmoreland was
the youngest first sergeant in the Army and would serve
three Vietnam tours with the 1st Cav. He was an extraordinarily talented gentleman and soldier. Although in considerable pain, he put on his no-nonsense, senior NCO face
and responded, "No damn problem, Sir. Garry Owen."

I cannot overstate the inner strength I was able to gain
from the first sergeant in that situation. We often assume
actual war mirrors what we see on the silver screen, and
that the natural thing for a man to do in times of great
combat stress is to act like a movie hero. Nothing could
be more distant from the truth. Some men freeze, some
curl up into a fetal position, and some run. A few, however, rise above the pain and the fear, grit their teeth and
keep on going. Noncommissioned officers the likes of
Sergeant Westmoreland understand that a critical compo-
nent of their job is to set, not just a good example, but a

*First Sergeant Haskell B. Westmoreland receives the
Silver Star Medal for gallantry in action.*

splendid example to the enlisted men and the officers alike,
particularly when the military chips are down. In this case
the Top did just that and, in doing so, strengthened my
resolve to get him and my other men out of the mess in
which we found ourselves.

"Say, Top," I deadpanned, "since you just have a little
pin prick there, how about keeping an eye out down the
end of this dike. If the bad guys get around there, we're
gonna be in deep trouble."

Without acknowledging the obvious understatement, he
responded matter-of-factly, "No sweat, Sir. I'll cover us."

As I crawled back towards the RTOs, I heard a yell from
the other side of the dike. Carefully, I peeked over, and
there, prone in the muck, was Rick Belt with a grim smile
on his face.

"Where the hell you been, Lieutenant?" I asked, returning the grin. I was delighted to see him.

"Just out for a swim. Where do you think?" he replied,

wryly. "Give us a hand. My sergeant's hit bad."

Behind him, submerged in the water with only his face showing, was Brent Hodges, flat on his back. Paul Riley, an extraordinarily courageous man, had heard Brent's call for help, found him, and pulled him from under the enemy's guns. Paul, on his stomach the entire way, had then dragged the man nearly fifty meters under fire. That was a herculean task, accomplished inches at a time. Just behind them came Rick Smith, pulling Brent's gear.

"Keep their heads down," I said to my men, who immediately opened up with rifles on automatic.

I jumped up over the dike and helped Rick pull the sergeant to safety. We propped the wounded NCO up on the side of the berm and opened his pants to reveal a nasty hole in his lower abdomen. Because the dike was so low, we could not elevate the sergeant's torso high enough to get the wound out of the water, and it oozed a thin stream of blood. When I looked back at him some minutes later, I could see ugly, black leeches wriggling up the blood trail towards the wound. Rick Belt was attempting to keep the leeches at bay. It was as chilling and repulsive a sight as I'd seen in Vietnam.

Years later Brent would tell me that he thought he'd been hit in the buttocks because ". . . that's where the pain was." He had no realization the bullet entered from the front and exited with a gaping wound through his derriere. When Sergeant Riley asked him where he was hit, Brent recalled, "I was embarrassed to tell my command sergeant I was shot in the ass, so I said I was hit in the belly, which was the truth, but I didn't know it."

Note must be made here that Richard Smith left my group after we jumped from the chopper, and proceeded on his own to rejoin his squad and try to rescue Sergeant Hodges. After we got Hodges to relative safety, Rick proved his mastery of the M-79 by taking the enemy under extremely accurate fire. "I remember shooting so many 40mm rounds," he said later, "that my right shoulder couldn't take anymore and, after being resupplied with ammo, I started firing left handed." It didn't make any difference which hand he was shooting with; Rick was most instrumental in keeping the enemy at bay while we resupplied ammo and organized for an assault on the village.

Awhile after we got Sergeant Hodges over the dike, the forward observer yelled, "Round on the way."

We were about to receive some indirect support at long last and, shortly thereafter, a 105 round landed just inside the village. Having seen the civilians exit the area, I felt comfortable with calling in a volley from the full battery. Three rounds crashed into the village just seconds later. The enemy fire slackened and my Third Platoon Sergeant told me later that one of the projectiles landed smack on top of an enemy bunker into which two NVA troops had scampered just moments prior.

As far as I was concerned, the battle was over and I ordered Doug McCrary to send me a squad with an M-60 for the assault on the village. I also asked John Long to send more ammo and a medic. I planned to rout the enemy with some minor adjustments to the big guns and two or three more volleys. The infantry assault would commence just as the rounds were about to impact and would put the finishing touches on a bad day. Unfortunately, my plans were not to be. The Old Man canceled the artillery in favor of some tactical air support he had requested earlier, when things didn't look so rosy. Although his decision under the circumstances was prudent and correct, I will spend the remainder of my life wishing I had been much more forceful in rejecting his decision.

About twenty minutes went by before two Air Force jets roared out of a leaden sky and flashed over the village. We were ordered to mark our positions. At the same time, the additional squad arrived, after a long duck walk behind the dike. I passed them the word about the air force. No one was happy, least of all the medic who made it very clear that Sergeant Hodges was not good and needed out of there fast.

We clearly marked our positions by throwing smoke

grenades forward of the dikes toward the village. I was at pains to have Colonel Swett make certain the pilots knew that some of Rick's men were nearly in the village, allowing no margin for error on the south side, and that Third Platoon's proximity to the huts gave the planes very little leeway on the west. Because Alpha Company was then somewhere north of the village, the fighters made their runs out of the west, so that any long bombs would land east of the huts, the only place where no friendlies were located. Unfortunately, a west-east run meant the fast movers would come in over Third Platoon's heads, and there was no way to move the Third back without exposing them in an open paddy to the enemy fire.

"Three Six," I radioed just before the first run, "get your men down in the water."

The first two pilots we saw that day were experts at ground support. They came in firing their cannons, the bombs were released just over the heads of the Third Platoon and the planes would cut in their afterburners and bank sharply left while climbing dramatically. The weapons would glide almost casually into the trees where they would disappear from sight, followed a second later by earth trembling explosions towards the rear of the village. That positioning meant, however, they accomplished little more than to make big holes in the ground.

With the planes gone I prepared to assault the village. The M-60 was set up on the extreme right side of our assault line to provide direct support. The four machine guns on the hill and the men in Third Platoon would give us covering fire from west to east. They would be able to engage the enemy almost to the time when the assault line entered the village itself.

I advised the Old Man we were ready to attack. Surprisingly, he said to wait. The air force had another aircraft which wanted to use up some unexpended ordinance from another mission. I requested he dump his load someplace else where it wasn't needed. Too late.

"Three Six, one more jet on the way. Mark your position and get down in the water."

Another jet screamed over our heads and banked left to come around for his ordinance run. I watched that guy all the way. When he released two bombs from beneath his wings, it was obvious they would be badly short of the target. The impact was exactly in the middle of Third Platoon, a direct hit. The results are locked in my memory to this day. The two black objects hit the water and then erupted, throwing men, weapons, helmets, grey muck and water in every direction. One man would eventually die of the wounds he received. Several others were badly hurt and evacuated to Japan. I never knew their fate. What spared the remainder of the squad was the fact they were well spread out and that the weapons were apparently fused to explode on contact, which they did in the foot deep mud beneath the water.

I do not recall grabbing the radio handset or much about what I yelled into it for all to hear. My RTOs tell me I threatened "to shoot that bastard down myself" if he made another pass. The battalion commander watched the entire disaster and was trying to calm me down while the S-3 attempted to call off the jet, to no avail. On his final run he released a napalm canister from under the belly of the aircraft. That time his release point was fine, but the six foot long weapon was on a cartwheeling trajectory to the extreme south side of the village where it struck the base of a palm tree in clear view of everyone behind the dike. Had the device detonated there it would have fried all of Rick's men and badly scorched the rest of us. That variety of palm grows in a graceful arc; the curve of the tree is most pronounced at its base, which is precisely the point where the canister struck. The trajectory was altered so that the weapon was simultaneously redirected upward about fifty feet and toward my group. I watched the cigar shaped, silver canister, realizing there was nothing I could do except yell "down in the water". Curiously, I didn't get down myself, but watched that terrible object ascend until it ran out of upward momentum and then settled downward, wobbling awkwardly; its length was parallel to the ground, not nose or tail first, when it struck the surface, producing a great splash. The flight of the canister from the base of tree to splash down took about five seconds. Accordingly, there was what seemed to be an eternity to watch what I knew was a device very capable of killing me. I was conscious later that my mind kept snapping in and out of that reality, one instant knowing I was going to burn to death and in another instant rejecting the thought, for no discernible reason other than a subconscious will to live. I ducked behind the dike for an instant as it hit and then popped up again. The weapon hit so close to my group that it splashed water over most of us and covered the First Sergeant with a layer of mud to boot. It did not detonate.

Bob Wolicki, trapped in the open paddy, would comment years later, "I don't remember much about what happened that day except for that giant, silver bomb which looked like it was hanging right over my head. It landed near where I was, but didn't go off."

Without waiting for a reply, I advised battalion I was assaulting. Several minutes later we were in the empty village. There was little more than burning huts, destroyed bunkers and some body parts.

I reorganized the company and moved out quickly, leaving John and Rick to evacuate our casualties. With A. J. Wise commanding Alpha Company on our left, restricting any movement toward the mountains, the enemy were forced to flee east through a lightly wooded area. On our right was a flooded paddy, miles in width, being patrolled by helicopter gun ships. No one could cross that expanse without being detected. Further east the Old Man inserted John Hitti with Bravo Company into a blocking position. For perhaps three of four kilometers, the NVA continued to engage us with sporadic sniper fire. When we were within a kilometer of Bravo's blocking position, the chase ended in a small village where my troopers captured eight men who were obviously soldiers. They were unarmed and had shed all their clothing down to their boxer shorts, but from their physical condition, uniform hair cuts, shoulder bruises where a gun would recoil, and marks on both shoulders indicating they carried heavy packs, we knew they were probably the guys we fought. A tough bunch, they would not, under questioning by ARVN interpreters, reveal where they had hidden their uniforms and weapons. They were North Vietnamese regulars.

Charlie Company relieved John Hitti in the blocking position where we were to set up for the night. Bravo flew out with the prisoners.

Just before dusk my RTO announced, "Resupply birds inbound." From the sound there were two aircraft, and shortly, one of the pilots came up on our frequency and asked if the landing zone was secure. "Yes," replied the RTO. "This time the LZ is secure."

The choppers were quite a sight. Every window, save the windshield, had a colorful cardboard turkey taped to it and the cargo area was much the same. On board was an enormous load of food, everything you could want to eat for Thanksgiving. Not long after, we were gorging on turkey with bread stuffing and cranberry sauce, mashed potatoes with gravy, green peas, fruit cocktail, cake with chocolate icing, juice, nuts, cookies, ice cream and hot coffee. There was more food than we could consume, even after the call went out for seconds and thirds.

Sitting there in the deepening gloom, I was struck with the absurdity of it all. Somewhere, not far off, there was a North Vietnamese battalion eating their typical evening meal of cold rice and water, while I feasted on hot turkey as if nothing was amiss. Two of my people were dead, four wounded, and an unknown number were injured from our own bombs. The top sergeant would be fine. Sergeant Hodges was questionable at that time.

The battalion commander had flown in earlier and told us we did a good job. We had. Charlie Company had captured the enemy and finally carried the day. To my mind, however, particularly because it need not have happened, we had won a decidedly Pyrrhic victory—a victory that simply cost too much.

Chapter 21

An Act Of War —
Paying The Cost

The woman lying on her back in the damp sand seemed to be looking right through me with lifeless eyes. She was without a thread of clothing on her. Normally the sight of that decidedly lovely, naked body would have stirred a need in me long neglected at the time, but months in the field produce an exhaustion which steals that desire. Her legs were spread apart, right knee slightly flexed, with her right hand over her breast and the fingers of the left resting on her pubic arch—as if she was making a futile attempt at modesty by concealing her private parts. A few long strands of hair snaked over her right shoulder and across her throat before meandering down toward her left breast.

The hair was wet and matted, and I surmised she must have been bathing in the river not long before. For nearly all Vietnamese there really wasn't any place else for attending to one's daily hygiene, certainly no tubs or showers with nice, warm running water They used the river which flowed out of the mountains.

Much of her coal black hair was scattered haphazardly over the sand. Normally, she would have tied her hair back in a bun, suggesting again that she'd been washing it before being interrupted.

Her body, a beautiful, light-almond shade except for the dark brown area around her nipples, was absolutely exquisite, a kind of sixteenth century exquisite that is. My impression was that the old masters drew a lusty, solid woman with emphasis on an overly proportioned beauty below the bust line; the woman in the sand was just that. Even as she lay there, her breasts were upright and youthful looking, but somewhat small and slightly out of proportion to her curvaceous hips which seemed to explode from her waist. Her thighs were overly generous, but with all that she wasn't overweight, just solid and muscular.

I mused about her physical appearance for a moment. Most of the Viet women I'd seen were rather on the thin side, hard and wiry, no doubt a product of the hard, farm life they led. My impression was this woman seemed heavier than most, but then I hadn't ever seen any Vietnamese woman in the buff, so I could have been wrong about their hidden physical attributes.

Looking at that woman, I couldn't help but think of my wife taking her own bath. She'd be in a tub filled with some sort of scented bath oil beads which made her smell delightful and the tub slippery as ice for the unsuspecting husband who might venture in soon after. I was thankful she was able to indulge herself without fear of some enemy soldiers intruding on her privacy.

The woman was in the southern portion of an unnamed valley near the Bong Song Plain, a reasonably secure area at the time, supposedly. The Cav had driven out most of the North Vietnamese and Viet Cong units known to frequent those environs; but our efforts certainly didn't do this lady a damn bit of good. Someone had intruded on her privacy with a vengeance.

What were the woman's feelings when she realized something very terrible was about to happen? I could imagine the gut-twisting, sickening fear. Her footprints were clearly visible where she emerged from the water and sprinted across a long sand bar in the shallow river, racing for the shelter of the trees at the riverside, probably glancing behind as she ran. Apparently, however, she soon understood that she wasn't going to make it and had turned to face her attacker. I envisioned the agonized, questioning, pleading look on her face — out of breath, rapidly gulping gasps of air while small, whimpering sounds escaped her throat, hands unconsciously attempting to cover her womanhood. She would be hoping against certainty that what was to be would not come to pass. But the tale recorded in the soft sand revealed she was hit and knocked violently backward, dead instantly. No, I mused angrily, my presence and the presence of the whole damn 1st Cav certainly didn't do her any good. This beauty on the sand before me was dead, the result of a violent act, in a war she most probably didn't know much about.

My thoughts were interrupted by a voice from behind.

"Nice pair of lungs. Wouldn't you say so, Sir?"

"Yes, Sergeant, a very fine set of lungs, indeed," I responded, without turning to the familiar voice standing behind me.

"Dead?" he said, more in the form of a statement to be affirmed rather than a question.

"Very," I answered.

The sergeant moved around me and bent over the prostrate form, looking at the hole in the top of her skull and the mess of gray brain tissue, blood, and bone fragments which had leaked out.

The sergeant looked saddened at the sight at his feet, perhaps thinking of his wife or a grown daughter somewhere back in the States. This sort of thing wasn't supposed to happen to a women. If she had a weapon, then you might justify her death; you could rationalize it if there was a weapon. Then, by definition, she is the enemy. She shoots at you, you shoot at her, and without much of a wait to see if the lady is going to pull her trigger first.

"Damn—what a shame," he said, then knelt on one knee and touched the woman's breast, squeezing it slightly. "Man, been awhile since I've had a hand on something as nice as that—still warm," he said with an admiring sadness, while slowly shaking his helmeted head.

"Ya know, Sir," he said slowly and thoughtfully as he stood up, looking again at the entry wound in the woman's head, "judging from the angle that slug must have gone into her head, she must have been hit by somebody shooting at her from above." Then the realization of what happened came to him and he said, "Damn. So this is what that chopper was shooting at."

We had watched the aircraft dip low over the river about three-quarters of an hour earlier, then make a quick turn and come back, its right door gunner firing his M-60 at something on the ground near the river bank. He was too far distant for us to clearly see any identifying markings. We assumed the chopper saw our company, but he didn't call for us to assist as would normally be the case if enemy troops were his targets. Curious, I had taken the sergeant's squad over to check the area out. We had spread out and had been looking along the bank for a few minutes before I discovered the woman in the sand.

Of course, there was the possibility that the chopper didn't shoot the woman. Almost every door gunner I'd ever seen liked to test fire his weapon from time to time, if for no other reason than to break the boredom. Obviously, however, the primary reason for checking the weapon was to insure it would be ready when the real thing came along; test firing was recommended and accepted as standard operating procedure. On more than one occasion, I'd been delighted to have the door gunners on our lift ships blast away at anything and everything on an LZ as we air assaulted in. Those M-60's were your very last covering fire before you hit the ground. Only once did I see one malfunction, and the look that the pilot gave the gunner left no doubt that the lad was in deep trouble. So, I had no doubt that many a log floating in the river had been targeted by chopper door gunners. Since the bird we saw shooting didn't call for us to mop up any VC that were the cause for his firing, the gunner may have just been testing the weapon; but the sergeant didn't see it that way.

"She must have run," he suggested. "Some of those guys think anybody who runs must be guilty of something. If they run, they're VC, fair game." He paused and then continued almost sadly, "A real shame, though. This don't look like NVA or VC; don't look hard enough, you know, like she's been toting guns or ammo down the Ho Chi Minh Trail. She looks more like a village frau." He hesitated and then, as if to reinforce his logic, added, "She's got no gun. There's her stuff right over there — no weapon with it."

I missed seeing the woman's belongings when I discovered the body. There were just the usual black pants, with a white blouse top woven of a finer see-through fabric, and a tight fitting undergarment. The clothing was neatly piled inside a coolie hat turned upside-down, with a pair of shower clogs beside it. If the woman was typical, these were most of her worldly possessions, I thought. My wife and I had a closet filled with clothes. That struck me as inherently unfair. Some have so much and some nearly nothing, and all based on the luck of being born in the United States versus Vietnam, or Thailand, or Cambodia, or most of Africa, or India, or a thousand other places. I looked again at the clothing. This was all she had except herself—her body and strength she used to make a living in the fields, her ability to bear children, her life—and now someone had taken all that from her.

The sergeant seemed lost in his thoughts for a few moments. Then I heard him sort of spit out a forceful but quiet "Damn", shaking his head. He paused briefly and made a weak attempted to justify the mess with the same tired, ineffective rationalization I'd heard time and time again. "Sir, this is a real damn shame, but better it happens here than back home. Wouldn't you say so, Sir?"

I didn't answer him immediately. The sergeant's men had arrived. They were gawking at the corpse, making various admiring or lewd remarks about her anatomy, reminding each other how long it had been since they'd seen a woman in that state of undress. I thought again of my wife, safe at home, secure in the knowledge that no helicopter gun ship would take her apart for the hell of it. How would I react if she were sprawled there? How could you reconcile this carnage with the rationale for our being in this war? If we weren't here, this murder would have never happened. However noble and correct the motive for being in this country, was our presence worth the loss of even this single innocent life?

The hour was late and it would soon be dark. The sergeant and I dragged the body over to her clothing on the river bank. I didn't want it to wash away overnight. We could, of course, dispose of the evidence by putting her in the river. The body would wind up downstream where it might or might not be fished out, in all likelihood unrecognizable. Just another body among many in a war. Vietnam wasn't like the United States; there wouldn't be an all-points bulletin for a missing woman, no exhaustive attempt to identify the corpse. There was scant chance anyone would ever know what really happened. Upstream, her clothes would be found, drowning suspected. The U.S. Army would be off the hook.

I rejected the idea. She should have a proper burial. Her family would come looking for her. They would bury her according to their religion and custom. That was the least I could do for her; that seemed the right thing. Let her people think what they would.

"You're wrong, Sergeant," I finally answered his question. "We can't allow it to be better if it happens here rather than at home," I said unconvincingly, because I didn't believe we could do much about it. "And, what's it gonna cost?"

"I don't get you, Sir."

"Well, what do you think any woman would do if she was skinny dipping in a nice mountain stream and some chopper loaded with a bunch of guys flew over her?"

"She'd run," he responded with a questioning expression, "for her clothes."

"Damn right, naturally she'd run," I said. "So did this woman, I'll bet. She was just taking a bath in a stream, minding her own business, washing her hair. She didn't have a gun, wasn't threatening anybody, let alone some jerk in a chopper. What kind of men have we created in this goddamned army who think its just fine to kill an unarmed, naked woman simply because she was running away? She was bare assed. What'd they think she'd do, piss on them or something? They could have landed and captured her if they thought she was a guerrilla."

My Irish was up by the time I got the last sentence out and I was nearly yelling at him. The sergeant seemed to sense my frustration and anger, but I'm not certain he comprehended. Here we were supposedly trying to make this country safe for women like this one now rotting at my feet, trying to act like human beings, while idiots like this chopper gunner were blowing away somebody's wife, some kid's mother, some parent's daughter. What would it be like to go looking for your wife who had gone to take a bath and find her brutally murdered? Imagine the anger when you find her body. Imagine the hate. How do you win a guerrilla war if your men are acting like that?

"This has got to cost, my friend," I said to him with an ugly vehemence. "I can't help thinking somebody's gonna pay for this—you, me, the whole goddamned army, the United States—somebody, something's gonna pay."

The sergeant was very quiet as we started to walk off. He seemed to be searching for something to say, something to counter my words, yet dispel my anger at the same time.

"I guess that's what happens in a war," was all he could come up with.

"Right, Sarge," I said sarcastically, nearly speechless with frustration, "just write it off as an act of war."

Two days later the sergeant was dead. Another act of war. I couldn't help wondering if he was the one who paid the cost.

Chapter 22

They Just Don't
Come Much Better

Charlie Company was traversing a particularly nasty bit of terrain, a very narrow tributary valley blanketed with heavy underbrush and topped with a thick leafy canopy. Movement on the floor of this particular defile wasn't overly difficult because of a fairly well-defined trail and a partially dry stream bed, along which the main body of my company was moving, with its platoons in column.

Maintaining adequate flank security was the major challenge, because the forward progress of the squads assigned that task was slowed significantly by the heavy brush and the steep sides of the valley; this caused the flankers to drift inexorably down slope, ever closer to the main body. Of course, as they came within earshot of the men on the valley floor, there was the danger of them being mistaken for the enemy. Our forward progress was slowed by the constant need to halt the company and reposition the flankers higher up on the hillsides.

At about 1100 hours, I called a rest halt. Bald Eagle Two, commanded by Doug McCrary, had been on point since about 0900 and they needed a break. Division Intelligence had warned us of the possible presence of a large North Vietnamese force thought to be in the vicinity. Our mission was to search out and destroy those NVA; since we expected to be out-gunned initially if we found them, the tension had built up to an extreme. Visibility through the thick underbrush was at a minimum; frayed nerves weren't helped any by an intermittent rain which soaked the troops to the skin and made it difficult to hear anything save the noise of the falling drops. The men on point were particularly susceptible to a build-up of tension in such situations and I liked to relieve them periodically. That was accomplished by passing the second, third and mortar platoons in the column through the first, when we moved out after a break, thus effectively changing those in the lead.

Another, much less deadly enemy we were facing that day was leeches. Technically described as a "chiefly aquatic bloodsucking or carnivorous worm", more often referred to as "the little bastards", the rain facilitated their getting up into the trees; as we moved along, everyone was plagued with the black, slimy creatures dropping off the leaves and landing on any warm-blooded body passing beneath. Once on you, they would work their way under your clothing, attach themselves to the skin, usually around your belt line or where your fatigue pants entered the top of your boots, and start sucking blood. Because their attachment was not painful, you had no idea they were there and doing damage until you looked.

The leeches weren't difficult to remove. Burning them off by placing the lighted end of a cigarette against their tail was effective, or you could pour some of the insect repellent we were issued on the repulsive critters. The bug juice didn't work worth a hoot on bugs, but it did a job on leeches. The repellent stung opened flesh, giving the impression it was disinfecting; invariably, however, the spot where they had attached themselves would become septic and be a bothersome nuisance. Best to get the creatures off before they attached themselves. To that end, it wasn't unusual, each time we took a break, to see men with their pants down, carefully examining their bare skin.

Since I was near where Doug McCrary was supposed to be located during the break, I decided to personally let him know about the pass-through. What I found was typical of what I had seen of my Two-Six. One trooper was certain he was up checking his men on the point. The fire team on point said he'd been there, but had gone to reposition his right flank. Yes, he had been on the right, but his platoon sergeant advised he was then over on the left.

Doug was a whirlwind of supervisory motion. Where others would utilize the radio, he did it in person and completely exhausted his RTOs, who had to trail him loaded, not only with their own equipment, but also with the PRC-25 and its attendant gear. I finally gave up the chase and advised him of the pass-through over the air.

Theoretically, passing one platoon through another is a piece of cake, but there is always somebody who doesn't get the word and screws things up. This operation was going to be made more difficult because, not only was the main body of the platoons going to pass through the lead platoon, but the flankers must do so at the same time. The platoon commanders were going to have to keep on their toes.

Having given the word to move out, I was walking with the First Platoon through LT McCrary's men when I saw Two-Six himself, fatigue pants and underdrawers down to his knees, clutching that appendage particular to the male of the species and jerking on it for all he was worth. I hardly need say that this sight was not what you'd expect in the depths of a hushed forest with an imminent NVA attack a real possibility. As the men quietly streamed past him, there were, of course, any number of whispered, good-natured, raw comments about the lieutenant's activities.

While the sight did break the tension a bit, obviously the lieutenant wasn't controlling his platoon at that critical moment, as I expected. For his part, Doug wasn't paying a bit of attention, but was bent over, intently examining himself. Suppressing a smile—difficult, to say the least—I interrupted, suggesting to the lieutenant that if he was overwhelmed with the need, he should consider delaying that activity for some more appropriate time.

The poor lieutenant, deadly serious, explained that when checking for leeches, he thought he saw one of the S.O.B.s slither into the opening of his penis. All this pulling and jerking was his attempt to get the little bastard out, but he'd had no luck to that point. Our medic didn't help any, because, without cracking a grin, the Doc ventured his medical opinion that a quick amputation was required before the leech got up into the bladder and caused all manner of life threatening problems. I'm certain Doug knew we were putting him on, but he still looked relieved when the Doc suggested, as an alternative, that the lieutenant take a large drink of water and urinate the leech out. Doug decided that was the preferable course of action and, with some apparent reluctance, let go, pulled up his pants, emptied his canteen and, with an embarrassed grin, got on with the mission.

I never did hear if there was really a leech in there, and we never did find any enemy that day, but the incident always enters my mind when I think of Doug McCrary. It was typical of his good natured openness and naivete which made him one of the best liked officers in the battalion.

Doug was a confederate boy from the Carolinas, with a not excessively pronounced, but very engaging southern drawl. I liked him a great deal, partially because that openness meant you never had to guess where he stood on any topic or decision; you could bet your bottom he'd tell you. He wasn't a tall man, but was broad at the shoulder and gave the impression of being physically powerful. Doug was almost never seen without a smile, no matter how bad the situation, and always had some wise crack about whatever adversity was at hand.

Eagle Two-Six was particularly devoted to his men and his platoon sergeant, a quiet, friendly and competent fellow named Flores. Doug, as I remember, was always trying to make sure his boys were well fed, adequately shel-

LT Doug McCrary with Montagnard child

tered when possible, and properly equipped. I recall once
seeing him at the end of a long wet day, with the rain
falling heavily, helping one of his men pitch a poncho tent
so he could get out of the wet. He looked after them
constantly when we were in the field, urging them to spread
out and not bunch up when we were on a march, checking
their weapons to see if they were clean, making certain
they were properly positioned for the night. He was a good
leader. First Sergeant Westmoreland, a man who had seen
more than his share of junior officers, uncharacteristically
lauded the lieutenant one day with, "They don't come much
better."

On February 16, 1967, the 5/7 Cav was being used as
a blocking force and ambush unit and was strung out across
thousands of meters with platoon, squad and fire team size
units operating almost independently. Bill Brown was in
command of Charlie Company by that time. He and I had
switched assignments and I was the battalion personnel

officer. At 1610 hours we received word from Bill that a portion of his Eagle Two unit was receiving heavy fire from a variety of small arms. Bill mustered a small reinforcing element and started to move toward his second platoon, a difficult march which took forty minutes. At 1651 hours he came under fire himself from an enemy force estimated to be ten to fifteen Viet Cong. In fact, there were many more.

By the time the reinforcements arrived, Doug McCrary's situation had deteriorated significantly. Operating with only two squads, and neither of those at full strength, his lead unit had been caught partially in the open by the first burst of enemy fire. Those men were heavily engaged and lying behind cover so sparse they were unable to return fire, and there weren't enough guns in the remainder of the platoon at that point to dislodge the enemy. Platoon Sergeant Flores was with that lead squad and was shot when he left a covered position in an effort to help his men get out of their untenable situation. After being hit, he was sprawled partially in the open, with the VC trying to finish him off.

Doug McCrary was directing the return fire of the remainder of his troops from a relatively safe, well covered position. When Sergeant Flores went down and it became obvious he was badly hit and unable to get under cover, Doug left his secure location and ran into the open after him.

Troopers who participated in the fighting recalled that when Lieutenant McCrary rushed into the open, the entire battle seemed to take a quantum leap in intensity. Each of the men with him ignored incoming rounds and were up blasting away at the enemy positions. The men who were pinned down realized the enemy had lifted their fire to shoot at someone else and took the opportunity to also engage the enemy.

"I was screaming and shooting, all at the same time," said one trooper later. "Everybody had one eye on the VC and the other on the lieutenant. We couldn't do much to help him, except keep the Cong's heads down, and for damn sure nobody was saving ammo."

For his part, Doug managed to reach his sergeant and, with an unbelievable display of courage, strength and determination, dragged him toward safety.

"Bullets flew all round him," recalled one man. "It was like every damn VC for miles around was sighting on his back. The lieutenant knew it, you could see it in his face, but he just kept pulling Sergeant Flores."

At 1656 hours the battalion headquarters recorded this radio message in the clear from Bill Brown: "Bold Eagle Six to War Paint. Still receiving fire. I have just lost my Second Platoon Leader."

First Lieutenant Douglas McCrary was killed instantly. Platoon Sergeant M. W. Flores was already dead.

They simply do not come much better.

Chapter 23

For The Good Of The Battalion

Food, ammunition, clothing, water and just about everything tangible needed to sustain a soldier in combat were the province of the Battalion Supply Officer, our trusty S-4. Captain Daniel David Crocket, "Davey" for short, held that post for the entire tour. He was a likable, serious fellow who did a better than adequate job for the troops in the field.

Our supply line to the battalion forward support facility where Davey was located started in the battalion rear, where Warrant Officer One Oscar W. Igoe held court. In the military, the officers are responsible for everything that gets done or fails to get done; but the sergeants and the warrants, experts at how the Army functions, actually get the work accomplished. Warrant officers rank just below officers and just above sergeants. They are not in the command line, but are specialists, support staff types. The S-4 is the gent who answers directly to the battalion commander. The supply warrant is his right arm, maybe both his arms. All warrant officers are called "Mister", except when they attain the highest warrant rank, Chief Warrant Officer Four. With that rank they are very respectfully referred to as "Chief".

Mister Igoe, was "up from the ranks", having been promoted from Staff Sergeant. As I was Battalion Adjutant and the rear area commander, Oscar was generally under my control, except in the technical aspects of supply. We got along well together. Our primary contact pertained to my job of getting replacement troops supplied with gear. I'd send the new men to Oscar's shop and he would send them back, loaded for combat.

Now, it is an indisputable fact of life in the military supply field that there is never a surplus of things you need. So, the supply folks make up any shortfall by utilizing the time honored method of "trading". In Vietnam, almost anything was fair barter and trading was epidemic. Flashlight batteries were traded for toilet paper, beer for ice, captured enemy weapons would get you just about anything you wanted from the desk warriors in the rear. Technically, all this is illegal, but then you didn't actually see it happen. Most of the items are "expendable", that is to say they are items expected to be used in the normal course of business. How much toilet paper a fellow uses is dependent on a number of things, and no one is counting the sheets. There is little harm in your trading a few extra batteries for some latrine paper. You can not, however, trade an M-1 tank for a 105mm howitzer, or thirty blankets for thirty poncho liners, because someone must physically sign and be accountable for such "nonexpendable" items. Many a man has personally reimbursed the government for nonexpendables he couldn't account for.

In the service, there is an elaborate system of accountability. However, accountability is less stringent in combat. "Trooper lost M-16, binoculars and helmet, when, through no fault of his own, he fell into a deep stream while in hostile territory:" that statement from the company CO will get the soldier, the platoon leader and the commander off the hook for all those items, even though the man's sergeant was heard to say, "The clown tripped over his own two feet and fell in the drink." Obviously, things get destroyed in combat. The bigger they are, however, the closer the accounting. It is not easy to write off a jeep or a tank unless the charred hulk has unfriendly holes in it.

One day I noted with some concern that in Mister Igoe's supply yard were no less than two aircraft engines. Now, there is no earthly reason why an infantry battalion could legally have aircraft engines. WO Igoe, in response to my inquiry, passed them off with a sly smile as "trade material". Two days later they were gone.

I felt obliged to relate my sightings to Davey Crocket whose career would be over if some curious military police had just happened by looking for those missing items. Dave confided to me that Mister Igoe required some watching and would be pleased if I would keep my eye on him. He said Oscar was selling PX packs on the black market in An Khe.

In combat, comfort items such as shaving cream, toothpaste, razor, cigarettes, cigars, chewing gum and candy were issued in what we called the PX pack. On an Army post, the corner store is known as the post exchange or PX. Thus, the boxes in which these comfort and morale items were delivered was the PX pack.

In the field we seldom could consume the entire contents of a PX pack. According to Dave, we had quite a surplus stockpiled with our friendly warrant officer who, conveniently enough, also kept the records on how many were expended. When asked to send a half-dozen forward, Oscar would note that eight went. The two others would then go to the black market in An Khe. Davey had given the warrant hell. "For the good of the battalion," Dave explained — "better that way."

As noted previously, officers are responsible for everything their men do or fail to do, and anything less than perfection is unacceptable. Careers have been lost because a PFC screwed up. Therefore, it is much better if misdeeds are taken care of internally, within the battalion or the company, as opposed to getting brigade or division into the act. "For the good of the battalion" simply means one doesn't want to disgrace the good name of the unit. Of course, left unsaid is the fact that the battalion commander's good name, or the company commander's, or the Supply Officer's are not besmirched either.

My opinion of Oscar was a bit shaken by the PX pack caper. All military supply people of my acquaintance possessed a little larcenous streak in order to survive. Small shortages of nonexpendables, such as spoons or bed sheets, was not uncommon, and replacing those items by "trading" wasn't unusual. Fortunately, Mister Igoe had not done anything to negatively affect the fighting troops. The PX packs were surplus. There would be a note in his record, perhaps; his efficiency report would be adversely affected, perhaps; Dave had taught him a lesson, perhaps.

In addition to the items in the PX pack, the lightweight poncho liner was the other treasured comfort item of the field soldier. As the name implies, the liner was made of a very light fabric, but one which provided an extraordinary amount of warmth. On the coast, temperatures exceeding one hundred degrees during the heat of the day were common, but it wasn't unusual for the night temperature to moderate markedly. Sweaty bodies and clothing cooled down considerably as the moisture evaporated. That poncho liner was just the ticket to keeping warm until the body could adjust. Very importantly, the liner was partially waterproof and, when wet, dried relatively quickly.

The liners were much prized by our Vietnamese friends also. Made from a silky fabric on which had been imprinted a green, jungle camouflage pattern, the Viets had their local tailor convert the liners into jackets—very useful and very much in vogue among the local military. Unfortunately, this made the poncho liners a much sought after item on the black market.

Late in our tour, the Fourth Division had some unpleasant experiences north of Pleiku, and our battalion was sent to reinforce them. That part of the Western Central Highlands was a very rugged, mountainous region, wet and cold at the time. Those factors combined to make the lightweight liner a real asset to the men in the field.

Nearly simultaneous to our move to Pleiku, the battalion started receiving large numbers of sorely needed replacements. As usual, Mister Igoe would equip the new personnel for combat. One day, however, as I inspected some new troops prior to their departure for their respective companies, I noticed everyone had the garrison-issue, wool blanket and not the lightweight poncho liner. That particular blanket was much heavier than the liner and it did provide warmth; but, when wet, the thing weighed a ton and never dried out, particularly under the conditions these men would experience. A call to supply and I was advised by Mister Igoe of a drastic poncho liner shortage throughout the Division. I told Oscar of the conditions these men were to face and he advised he would try to get some liners. Several days later, another group of replacements, more wool blankets, no liners. I suppose I could be accused of possessing a nasty bent of mind, having no real reason to disbelieve Mister Igoe's story. Nonetheless, my suspicions were aroused.

With Oscar at Division Headquarters soon thereafter, I visited his supply shop in which worked a staff sergeant and a PFC. No liners were in sight, but as soon as I asked a question about them, the sergeant started to ease away from me and the topic. The PFC, a handsome young man from Puerto Rico named Ruiz, became very nervous. I asked them tactfully if anything untoward was occurring with regard to the poncho liners. They professed no knowledge of any misdeeds.

My mistake, of course, was speaking to them together. Later that day, PFC Ruiz surreptitiously visited my office. He explained that WO Igoe was selling the poncho liners on the black market in An Khe. He had Ruiz write off dozens of them as lost in combat. In addition, he had some of the unsuspecting replacement personnel, in the usual rush and confusion of getting their combat gear, sign for liners they were never issued, thus overcoming the accountability problem. He would then stuff liners into laundry bags, haul them into town with the regular laundry run, and sell them to the laundry man. Ruiz, who served as Oscar's driver, had witnessed the entire operation several times. Oscar's deeds went undetected until he got greedy and sold all the liners he had. When we were hit with the rash of new replacements, he couldn't supply them.

A number of Vietnamese laundry establishments thrived in An Khe. The First Cavalry had its own mobile laundry unit as did all Army divisions. Unfortunately, clothes would come back very wrinkled because the laundry platoon didn't press anything. What would you expect in a war? Well, what one would logically expect and what some generals liked to see were two different things altogether. The division commander wanted a starched and pressed uniform, so he would look good in case someone of importance came to visit. Since the major general was all spiffy, the brigadier couldn't look any less, and the colonels had to look the part, and so on down the ranks. The Vietnamese, astute business people that they are, started laundries which would not only wash the uniforms, but starch and press them. Therefore, one sent underwear, socks and the like to the laundry platoon, and outer uniforms to town. Mister Igoe hauled the laundry—a very convenient arrangement.

With the information that Oscar was selling the poncho liners on the black market, I found myself in a quandary. Mister Igoe, in spite of everything, was a very engaging fellow and I didn't really want to ruin his career. At the time, I didn't feel I could confront him directly with the information Ruiz had given me, for fear he would make life miserable for the PFC. I decided to give him another chance to shape up and fly right. When a new group of replacements arrived, I made a specific point of telling Mister Igoe of the terrible conditions in the field and the need for the lightweight liners. I asked him to make a special effort to supply these new men with them. I even made an oblique comment that perhaps there were some "irregularities" in the supply chain which, if discovered, would be dealt with severely. It didn't work. The new men reported to me with wool blankets, and PFC Ruiz advised me that our warrant was about to take another shipment of liners to town the following day.

At that point I was particularly angry. I started to call Davey Crocket, but rejected that option. He would have to investigate. Mister Igoe would deny everything and, very importantly, have the paperwork to back himself up, and PFC Ruiz would be in trouble with the warrant and his sergeant. At best, I thought, Crocket would report it to the Old Man, who would also lack proof, and Igoe would get off with another slap on the wrist.

I must emphasize, that was the way one played the game—through the chain of command. A good team player would proceed that way and keep his own rump out of hot water. That was simpler and personally safer. However, by my standards, Mister Igoe had already been forgiven one serious indiscretion in the PX pack incident. I felt, rightly or wrongly, the Old Man wasn't about to air this dirty laundry in front of the Division since the case would be, essentially, the word of PFC Ruiz against Igoe's. "For the good of the battalion-" would be invoked. However, I viewed Oscar's actions as directly affecting the fighting performance of the men in the field. To me that was the cardinal sin.

I decided to advise the military police of Mister Igoe's actions. The Criminal Investigation Unit agreed to trail him the next time he went on a laundry run; I needed only to alert them by phone when I was certain a black market transaction was to take place.

About 1300 hours the next day, I received a hurried call from Ruiz. Igoe was making a run with liners almost immediately. A few minutes later, I saw the warrant's jeep with Ruiz at the wheel coming down the road. I stopped him and asked what he had in the jeep—"laundry". Had he made any progress on getting liners? There were "none to be had". I went over my litany about how bad the men would fare in the field without the liners. Mr. Igoe "couldn't help"; he "was doing all he could".

Oscar was looking me square in the eye and lying un-abashedly. My choices were clear: grab the liners I knew were in the jeep and haul Igoe to the Old Man, or call the MPs which almost assuredly would lead to a court-martial and a finish to the warrant's military career. Even at that late hour both were real possibilities.

I called the military police who trailed him to An Khe and caught him red-handed in the laundry; the poncho liners were there also. Unfortunately, they did not actually see him pass the liners to the Vietnamese laundry man. The case against him would hinge on sworn statements from PFC Ruiz and myself, and the circumstantial evidence of the liners in the laundry.

I was called to the Provost Marshall's Office later that day to fetch him. He was crying and, judging from his puffy, red eyes, had been for some time, but I didn't feel the least bit of compassion for him. The military police had not said a word about how they knew of his black market activities and I didn't tell him either. He found out, of course.

"Why did you do it, Bernie," he asked. "I thought we were friends. You tryin' to get some career points on your record?"

"We were friends, Oscar," I answered. "And how many times did this friend ask you about a shortage of liners? How many chances do you get? First one you got was with the PX packages." There was a look of surprise on his face which told me he didn't realize I had knowledge of that event. "You know the old saying: 'First mistake is on me. Second one is on you.' Well this was yours, Mr. Igoe. And," I added as an afterthought, "I'm not gonna get any career points for this one, my friend. You know as well as I that no one is going to award me any merit badge."

He knowingly shook his head in the affirmative.

"Then why'd you do it?" he questioned again.

"For the good of the men. For the guys out in the boonies with a wet blanket. You wouldn't know because you've been back here in the rear in relative comfort and safety. They're the reason. Good Lord, man, we've shipped fifty or sixty good soldiers home in boxes already. Don't you think they deserve some comfort before they're zipped into a body bag?"

Perhaps I wasn't making much sense and I searched his face for some hint of understanding, but found none. The impression I received was that he was thinking only of himself.

My departure from Vietnam came before Mister Igoe faced a court-martial. He was forced to remain in-country beyond his normal return date to the United States. I wasn't privy to his fate until years later when I learned he spent a good deal of time in the military stockade at Fort Leavenworth, atoning for his deeds.

Chapter 24

The Holy Man

"Protestant holy man's on his way, Bern. Wants to hold a service. Can you round up some bodies?"

John Hitti would normally announce the impending arrival of one of our two chaplains in just that manner, usually with an exasperated look on his face. Only occasionally was Bravo Company in a secure, fixed position long enough to allow a chaplain to hold a formal worship service. John's frustration resulted from the fact that he and I felt some obligation to turn out a decent congregation, so that the priest or the minister would feel his efforts were appreciated. With nearly 120 men getting their fannies shot at periodically, logic would dictate there would be no dearth of churchgoers. Not so. I would have to nearly dragoon men into attending the service in order to even approach a respectable number of worshipers. I suppose that relates to the eternal optimism of youth. Nearly everyone there thought himself a Superman—no bullet had his name on it. As a result, much of the time I was embarrassed at the number of men who attended the service, perhaps ten for Protestant services, half again as many for Catholic Mass.

To me, a chaplain at work in the Vietnam bush was a confusion of symbols, contrasts, and contradictions. The country is lush, green and truly beautiful; but irregularly across its face there are ugly scars of bare earth, dusty landing zones and fire bases gouged violently into the landscape—an area of craters, bunkers and shattered tree stumps. The country is underdeveloped, yet invaded by the most highly developed, powerful nation on earth, possessing all the trappings of warfare gone high-tech. Into that mix of beauty and the destruction which defiles it comes the chaplain. Apparently, he is necessary. This most powerful nation, which proclaims "In God We Trust", does not trust its God to rightfully settle a dispute among men. The nation which purports to follow the commandment "Thou shalt not kill", is doing just that. Therefore, the chaplain is required to legitimize the violent death, to vest mayhem with righteousness, to connect death with truth and goodness. He is there, in part, to remind us that we are The Good. The enemy, the Communist and therefore the Godless, is The Evil. Remorse at having killed is, thereby, rendered unnecessary; death at the hands of the enemy has a purpose, is given worth.

Throughout the service the contradictions continue. The chaplain finds something on which to place his portable altar topped with its wooden cross, but too often that item of worship is placed on a pile of munitions boxes. Catholic Mass has been celebrated on the fender of an 8 inch, self-propelled howitzer. The chaplain sings a hymn amid the hollow, metallic clang of an artillery piece fired nearby and the shriek of the outgoing round.

The man of God stands in jungle fatigues and combat boots. He has removed his combat helmet. The only semblance of clerical vestments is a long black stole draped about his neck, hanging to his knees. The stole is the symbol of his ecclesiastical authority. On each of its ends are symbols. A cross, the symbol of Christianity, is there and below the cross and juxtaposed to it is a fierce American eagle with an olive branch in one talon and war arrows in the other. The symbols seem to say: remember God and his admonishment to love thy neighbor, but don't forget the mission. The cross and the eagle are embroidered in gold, a mark of wealth, and they come to a country as desperately impoverished as it is beautiful.

The sermon begins for the few who come. The chaplain tries to make you feel comfortable with what you are doing. The message is not "get out there and kill the heathens", but more an attempt to reassure you that our side is in the right; we're doing our duty—God will bless that effort. I can't help but think about the men we are fighting. What about their God? I doubted that everyone in the North Vietnamese Army or the Vietnamese National Liberation Front were atheists. To what deity do they pray? Who is helping them? I look at the symbol of our country on the chaplain's stole, recall the motto "In God We Trust", and question again for what we are trusting Him. I have a sheet of paper in my hands titled: "Order of Service, for the Worship of Jesus Christ", and I'm cradling an automatic rifle in my lap. Is that trust? Something seems very wrong.

Chaplain (MAJ) Thomas Widdel saying mass at his makeshift altar, LZ English, May 1967

Our resident man of God was Chaplain Thomas Widdel, called Father Tom by all, regardless of rank. He was a Roman Catholic priest. If you needed personal counseling in the 5/7 Cav you talked to the priest. Unless the problem was specific to a particular religion, for personal difficulties there were no denominations; you got the guy assigned to your unit.

Father Tom was in his mid-forties, I would guess, physically imposing yet gentle of manner, a major, career Army, but you wouldn't know it. A quiet introspective man, I had the impression he was actively wrestling with the obvious conflict represented by a man of God present in a war. I never did, but often wanted to, ask him how he reconciled the fighting and the hatred with peace and forgiveness; how he could espouse the admonition to "Love Thine Enemy" while his flock was actively killing other human beings.

During my tenure as the Battalion Adjutant, Father Tom and I worked closely together. Our joint tasks dealt with the bottom line of war—tending to and accounting for the wounded and the dead. At that time, the 5/7 Cav support area was located at LZ English where the good padre had his tent pitched permanently. Word that one of our units had taken casualties would be radioed to the battalion tactical operations center at any time of the day or night. Medevac was requested by the TOC and casualties went directly from the field to Company B, 15th Medical Battalion at English. From there the seriously wounded would be flown to surgical hospitals at An Khe or Qui Nhon. Humanity required that someone meet the wounded and offer them encouragement. The Army system of accountability dictated that someone look after their personal belongings and military equipment. Army regulations also required at least two individuals positively identify the dead. The chaplain asked me to let him know when medevacs were coming. He wanted to be there and I was grateful for his help. The tasks were often very unpleasant.

The job was made more difficult because we seldom knew the names of those being evacuated, whether they were wounded and if so how badly, or if they were dead. Medical evacuation in Vietnam was so rapid, and the medevac crews on the choppers so courageous, that many casualties were flown out while the unit was still under hostile fire. In the 1st Cavalry, platoons were often widely separated. The company commander, who was the radio link between the platoon and medevac at battalion, sometimes didn't know the identity or condition of the injured and could only radio the location and the number of men to be lifted out. Accordingly, Father Tom and I often took the short jeep drive to the 15th Med with a sense of foreboding, not certain just what to expect.

Normally, the chaplain's face was seldom absent a smile. On the ride to meet a medevac he was a different person, grim-faced and quiet. No time for small talk.

"Whatta we got, Bernie?" That was all he'd say.

Medical priority dictated that the most seriously wounded would be flown out first. Therefore, if the first chopper disgorged men who were ambulatory, we could heave a sigh of relief, knowing that we had a good chance of not getting anyone more seriously injured. With that knowledge I could see the strain ease on the chaplain's face. If they came on a stretcher and were serious, he'd try to speak to them before the doctors went to work. While the Padre was doing that, I would collect what gear and weapons they came in with, and tag those items for storage.

Of course, if there was no question that a soldier was KIA, his body would be flown out after all the wounded had been evacuated. When a trooper arrived dead, it was always a shock. As soon as an obviously dead body was hauled off the chopper, Father Tom would give an almost involuntary negative shake of his head, as if trying to will that the thing hadn't happened. "Kilo india alphas" were particularly difficult for the two of us because someone, usually both of us, had to identify the remains.

For some reason, we seldom spoke of individuals killed in action as being "dead". We always chose to refer to them as kilo india alpha, the military phonetic alphabet for the letters K, I, and A, meaning killed in action.

"We have two kilo india alphas coming in, Sir." That would be the way tragedy was announced. Never did you hear, "We have two dead men." I suspect that was the case because, deep down inside us, we didn't like to acknowledge or speak of the reality of death.

The Graves Registration Unit was easily recognized because of the refrigerated truck trailer which stood behind the last tent in the hospital complex. The trailer was the storage facility for the bodies until they could be flown to Saigon. The heat and humidity in that tropical country were such that corpses decomposed rapidly and had to be kept cold. One day we saw a KIA, who had been killed about thirty hours previous, brought into the GR Unit. The man had lain in an open field under a broiling sun until his company could beat off the NVA. A physically large man to begin with, in those hours the body had swollen nearly three times its size. I doubted it could fit into a body bag until the gases created by the decomposition had somehow dissipated.

In front of the trailer was a large field tent. In its interior the only furniture was a portable field desk with a chair near the entrance and a large pile of body bags at the far end. Bodies awaiting ID and processing would be laid out on the bare ground in the black, rubber bags; they looked something like a thin rectangular sleeping bag with a zipper up the middle and four looped handles at each corner. Sometimes there were rows of filled body bags lined up.

The first ID was mine to make, assuming I knew the man well enough. From his dog tags, the Graves Registration people could usually get name, rank, and serial number. The GR boys would then cross-check my verbal identification with the information on the dog tags. The names always matched because I wouldn't make an identification unless I was absolutely certain. The consequences of making a mistake were too great to screw up. Ideally, within twenty-four hours of a positive identification, a KIA's next-of-kin would be notified. I definitely didn't want someone's wife or family being erroneously informed of his death. In the event there were no dog tags, I carried a roster of all our men in the battalion. From that I could get preliminary information, assuming I could make the ID. Because I had served in Bravo, Charlie and Headquarters Companies, I knew a great number of the men in the battalion. However, sometimes I would have to call for the personnel clerk or supply sergeant from the dead man's company to help with the identification. On one rare occasion I had to have a man brought in from the field to identify a new replacement who had been with the battalion just six hours before he was killed. If Father Tom didn't know the individual, I'd get busy and round up one or two men who could positively identify the deceased.

Ideally, the identifications were made independently. Therefore, after I made the first ID, the chaplain came in to make the second. The task seemed particularly devastating for that man of God, of peace and of love to even enter the Graves Registration tent, but he did, time and time again. The GR people would open the back of the tent to let in some natural light, zip open the bag just enough to expose the face, and let Father Tom take a look. He'd do so, have a word of prayer or give the Last Rites of the Church to Catholic men, and then give that involuntary shake of his head as he left.

Frequently, the identification was not easy. Men who die violently are often difficult to recognize. That difficulty resulted not just from the fact that their facial features might be totally or partially destroyed, but often a man's face would be contorted and frozen in an unnatural pose, particularly if he had suffered greatly. Additionally, we viewed the body lying flat in a bag. I was amazed how dependent one is on seeing the entire person, alive and standing, talking and animated, in order to recognize him.

Occasionally, a doctor would be in the GR tent with us. He was obliged to officially determine a reason for the man's demise for the death certificate. The discussion between the doctor and the Graves Registration sergeant, concerning a person who was alive and easily recognizable only a short time before, always sounded overly clinical, cold and unfeeling. The presence of the doctor evoked a dread in me. Up to the point when the doctor signs the death certificate, a human being exists. Life is officially gone with that signature; a person is no longer—he has become a statistic.

One day the chaplain and I had to identify a particularly fine platoon sergeant we both knew very well. The sergeant had been one of my best men when I commanded Charlie Company. He had been commanding the platoon and fell victim to a remotely detonated mine. Witnesses observed that a number of our men had passed the site of the explosive without setting it off. Nothing happened until the sergeant and his RTO, with the telltale radio antenna, approached. The VC must have been watching and didn't blow the device until the guy nearest the radio man was on top of it. As we entered the Graves Registration tent, a doctor in rubber gloves was kneeling beside a body bag filled with what looked like chopped meat. The doctor was at great pains to identify the body parts, so thoroughly was the man destroyed.

He picked up a chunk of flesh and bone about the size of a loaf of bread. "Piece of upper leg," he said to the Graves Registration man who was waiting for nothing more than a cause of death.

The doctor seemed mesmerized by the bloody pieces and continued to sift through the mound of flesh in the bag. I presumed he was attempting to insure that he had a human before him and not something else. Legally he was responsible for declaring a human being dead. I thought about my men in Charlie Company gathering up all those pieces. Must have been tough. An identifiable part was pulled out of the bag—a right hand and wrist minus two fingers and parts of the others.

After what seemed forever, the doctor decided that the platoon sergeant died from massive trauma. I glanced at

Father Tom. The priest had a pained expression on his face, eyes closed, partially turned away from the gore. I thought he was praying, but what would you expect. I suggested to the Graves Registration man that we couldn't be of much help on the ID, but that we would arrange for witnesses to be flown in from the field to attest to the identity. He agreed with a shake of his head and we left.

The year continued that way, a series of tragedies to be counseled, encouraged or identified. The chaplain was there through it all. At times my duties took me back to An Khe. As a result, I missed some of the KIA identifications. He saw them all.

Someone has said that war has an ennobling effect on a few and a ruinous effect on many. I believe that with Father Tom the conflict was ennobling; when his time came to leave that place after one year and go back to peace and some civility, Chaplain Thomas Widdel extended his tour in Vietnam for another year.

"The men need me here," was the reason he gave to me.

I believe they did.

Chapter 25

Lucrative Target

Surrounding the 1st Cavalry main base is the expanse of wilderness the French dubbed the grands vides—the great empty spaces. That vastness was an excellent staging area for attacks on Highway 19 and Camp Radcliff, the 1st Cavalry main base at Ah Khe.

In this same area during the French-Indochina War, a reinforced regimental combat team composed of infantry, armor and artillery battalions—the famed Mobile Group 100—was destroyed in a bloody ambush. Two years before our arrival, a Vietnamese convoy was savagely mauled in the same spot.

For a time, the mission of the 5/7Cav was to patrol a portion of that expanse north and west of An Khe, in an attempt to preempt any enemy mischief. The old adage that the best defense is a good offense applied in this case. Concomitantly, our tactical gurus were well aware of Ho Chi Minh's guerrilla philosophy which dictated how the NVA and VC were conducting the war:

If the tiger stands still, the elephant will crush him. But the tiger will not stand still. He will leap upon the back of the elephant, tearing huge chunks from his side, and then he will leap back into the dark jungle. And slowly the elephant will bleed to death.

Therefore, we sent a single company abroad in that wilderness, hoping it would present a lucrative target and lure the tiger out of hiding, anxious to repeat the victories of years prior. The remainder of the battalion with helicopter transport were waiting, however. If the tiger pounced, we would kill him.

The dominant terrain feature in our sector of those empty spaces was a continuous line of low hills which ran approximately north-south. We soon discovered that our company operating on the western side of those elevations was out of effective radio contact with supporting artillery and the battalion operations center at Camp Radcliff. To remedy the problem, a small landing zone was carved into a hill which was the highest point along the line of elevated terrain. It was utilized as a radio relay station and as a staging area for friendly units who would fly in and proceed into the bush on foot.

For the last three days the LZ was in operation, I was ordered to command the facility and the small unit defending it. Left unsaid when I was given the assignment was the fact that a such a lonely outpost might prove a tempting target. Nonetheless, I was pleased to get away from the Adjutant's desk for a time and back out in the field.

I arrived to find the place was a mess from a tactical perspective. The actual defensive perimeter was less than thirty meters wide and extended along the hill for nearly one hundred meters. Because the landing zone was absolutely flat, an enemy machine gun could rake the defenders on either side with grazing fire from the tree lines on the north or the south ends. To top it all off, someone located the command and radio relay bunker on the north end of the LZ, and then cleared the trees to the south for about one hundred and fifty meters. But for some reason which defied logic, they only cleared the trees north of the dugout for about forty meters. Some Charlie with a good arm could chuck a grenade nearly that far.

The security force was a composite unit comprised of

squads from several companies in the battalion. The senior NCO was a mortar platoon sergeant. Including myself, Nguyen the interpreter, and two RTOs, there were just about two squads to cover a perimeter that was nearly indefensible.

To beef up our forces, I had a newly arrived platoon of Vietnamese Regional Force/Popular Force soldiers, otherwise known as RF-PF, or more commonly and sarcastically—Ruff-Puffs. A quick head count of the RF-PF platoon produced just two full squads. These troops were charged with half the defense of the landing zone. When I arrived, they were all nestled together in a couple of elongated dugouts on the western side of the perimeter in various states of undress, smoking and generally goofing-off. Nobody appeared to be on guard. Their commander, a Vietnamese first lieutenant, was sitting in the shade of a poncho that covered part of the dugout, laughing and smoking with several of his men. Their U.S. advisor, a nervous artillery captain, was with them.

"Real good men," he confided. "Their CO, the lieutenant there, is a relative of the An Khe District Chief. Real good men."

"You camping out here with them?" I inquired.

"Ah—well—no—don't think I can. Real good men, though. You'll like them," was his hesitant answer. "Matter of fact, here comes my chopper now."

He look relieved as he boarded the bird for his flight back to a safer place. How did he know if they were good or not? Difficult assessment from thirty kilometers away.

Our major problem was that extreme north end of the LZ. There, some genius had allowed a dugout position to be built about twenty-five meters from the wood line. It was a wide, relatively shallow depression compared to a proper fox hole, with a few sand bags thrown up around it stacked two high. This was the key fighting position for the entire defensive perimeter. If an attack were to come, I was betting the unfriendlies would launch their effort from that tree line, where a force would be concealed until its final assault over the thirty or forty meters of open ground. That single emplacement was the only one facing those threatening woods, with the exception of the command bunker itself. The obvious solution was to clear the trees and underbrush on the north end, but no explosives were at hand and I couldn't get more, due to the fact that the LZ was to be abandoned in a matter of days. Considerably mucking up an already bad situation was the fact that the position was occupied by a lone RF-PF—but not your ordinary Ruff-Puff.

Regional Force-Popular Force units were ill-equipped, ill-trained, ragtag outfits, officered by men who bought their rank or obtained it by virtue of a relationship with someone in the government. I wasn't keen on turning the Achilles Heel of my perimeter over to some untested RF/PF, and set about correcting the situation.

As I approached the position, up from the hole popped a Vietnamese soldier. This guy was just five feet tall, if that. He looked ancient for this kind of fighting, carried the rank of sergeant on his sleeve, and had a scarred and deadly serious face. In the position, pointing toward the woods, was an old Browning Automatic Rifle of World War II vintage. From his stern countenance, I received the impression this guy was out here for a serious purpose, an important job. He was, as a matter of fact, the only Ruff-Puff pulling any kind of guard duty on their portion of the line.

However well-intentioned the man was, there was no way I could let his butt hang out there, primarily because my butt and every other man's on that landing zone relied too heavily on that position. My plan was to place one of our machine guns in tandem with this guy's BAR. I wanted to construct two positions just forward of the command dugout on either side. That would move the BAR back about ten meters or so, out of grenade range. I believed that would keep him happy and solve my problem. I couldn't allow him to stay so close to the woods, not to mention the fact that he would be in the machine gun's line of fire if he remained there.

Fortunately for me, Nguyen had been sent along to be our interpreter, allowing me to communicate, second hand, with the Ruff-Puff sergeant.

"Nguyen, tell the sergeant his position is too near the woods and I'd like him to move it back toward the command bunker."

(Vietnamese chatter between Nguyen and the RF-PF.)

"Sir," said Nguyen, "He say he can no move gun."

"Why not? He's too close to the woods. Some VC's gonna hit him in the chops with a grenade."

(Extended Vietnamese chatter between the two.)

"Sir, he say no."

"What's his problem, Nguyen?"

(More Vietnamese chatter. Nguyen looks disturbed, perplexed.)

"Sir, he say he cannot take orders from me. I am sergeant, younger than him. He is old man. He know all about war."

"Nguyen," I was getting exasperated, "tell the gentleman—very respectfully—that I very much admire his great knowledge of war, but tell him he's going to get killed if we are attacked from the woods, and be sure he realizes I am telling him, not you. OK?"

(Chatter. Nguyen gets mad and a shouting match ensues.)

"Sir, he say he will not take orders from me. He say his lieutenant put him there and the dai uy," (the advisor who just flew off with other things to do), "say this position OK, numba one."

"Nguyen, you tell him this dai uy," pointing to the captain's bars on my uniform, "wants him to move it."

(Heated chatter.)

Nguyen shook his head with a mad, defeated look on his face. You could tell he had been working hard to make the guy understand, but to no avail. At that moment I was glad I wasn't an advisor to some ARVN outfit. Obviously, the Ruff-Puff sergeant knew who outranked whom and was perfectly aware that Nguyen was only speaking for me—but even I was much younger. Therefore, he was correct, not me. I had just been given a lesson in oriental protocol.

I briefly toyed with the idea of having the sergeant's platoon leader come over and give his BAR man an order to move the gun emplacement, but thought better of it. The lieutenant had been witness to the event from a distance not great enough to miss the conversation, and hadn't volunteered his assistance. Someone would lose a good deal of face if he were drawn into the conflict at that point. That someone was apt to be me.

"Platoon Sergeant," I yelled, walking back from the BAR emplacement about ten meters further from the tree line to a spot left of the command dugout.

"Yes, Sir."

"Sergeant, I want you to have an M-60 dug in right here to cover that tree line. Have your men do a good job of sandbagging it in. It'll be the key to our defending this place if Charlie comes at us from the woods."

"What about the Ruff-Puff, Sir? When the gun swings right, we'll be shooting right into his head if he gets up too far."

"That's his problem. I can't risk the rest of us so he can have his way; and Sergeant, when he does move out of the way for a minute to get some chow or take a leak, have your boys test the gun. I'd like them to lay some fire into those woods every so often to keep any VC from getting too close. I hope our Ruff-Puff will get the message."

The new M-60 emplacement was dug and sandbagged in a few hours. The Ruff-Puff held his ground until chow time when he left with his weapon. The gun test started shortly thereafter and, in doing so, my gunner dropped his point of aim, as if by accident, and tore up a good many of the sandbags surrounding the BAR man's fighting position. He never returned to the hole.

As darkness began to fall, I registered some artillery concentrations around the perimeter, with particular emphasis on that critical northern end. The Ruff Puffs started to look very nervous as I bracketed the artillery rounds on to the ridge line. They were not at all accustomed to live artillery flying in like a freight train over their right shoulders and impacting with a roar just seventy-five meters to their front.

The night was miserable—just dark enough to make vision difficult, but light enough to turn every bush into an enemy soldier. The wind was very calm, a good night for sounds. Normally I don't spook easily, but I was certain the VC were out there. We were so certain of activity at the edge of the woods, I called in artillery illumination rounds on two occasions. About an hour later, we fired two of the claymore mines out in front of the command bunker.

Through all that, the Ruff Puffs were particularly quiet and, fearing they were asleep, at 0200 I slipped over to their position. Everyone of them was in the Land of Nod except for the BAR man. I made a mental note to sing that guy's praises when I got back to base, and went over to sit next to him. He didn't acknowledge me at all, nor I him. We simply sat side by side for ten minutes looking into the blackness before us.

Just before I departed, I tapped him on the back, pointed and whispered, "You number one soldier."

I thought I caught just a trace of a smile cross his face. Then I took a grenade from my belt, showed it to him, pulled the pin and casually dropped it just outside of their bunker. The proximity of the explosion did a job on those sleeping beauties. I doubt they closed an eye afterward.

I was happy to see the dawn. I continued the machine gun fire into the woods at odd times throughout the day and sent out a patrol at 1600 hours, with orders to reconnoiter out at least five hundred meters. They reported back that a trail which ran along the spine of the ridge was showing signs of recent use. Later I received word we would abandon the landing zone early the following day.

The night was reasonably quiet in contrast to the one previous, the result, perhaps, of my quick use of the artillery. When the machine gunner thought there was movement to his front on the north, I called in my preregistered concentration and walked high explosives right down to the edge of the woods. I think the VC, if in fact they were out there, got the word.

The world was peaceful after that and I took a break outside the bunker in an effort to keep awake. In all probability, this would be my last opportunity to command in a hostile environment. I had looked forward to it, quite forgetting the hardships, not the least of which was the lack of shut-eye. I mused over the tremendous amount of destructive power I had just unleashed on the hilltop. Was there something pleasant about that ability? Was there something challenging about the cat-and-mouse death game of trying to outwit the enemy? Was there something ego inflating about having the authority to command men? At that moment all seemed well and the answer to those questions was yes, but just for the moment; because I knew, in the final analysis, there was no joy in having combat command. The horrors commanding troops in combat are real and permanent, the good aspects fleeting, if not imaginary. To comprehend the bad you need only ask those who have had that power, authority, and responsibility. To discover the good you need only find someone who has not commanded and still seeks it. With a last look at the thousands of twinkling gems in the black void above me, I stole back to the death game.

On the first sortie next morning, we had just enough lift ships to get the RF-PF out as a group. They seemed delighted to leave. After they were gone, we destroyed our positions.

Off that lift of incoming choppers came a five man, stay-behind patrol led by a buck sergeant, well-known as an effective leader of a long range reconnaissance patrol (LLRP). Often a LLRP would set up an ambush at a newly abandoned LZ, anticipating VC scavengers visiting the site. Prior to our departure, after informing me of his mission, the sergeant and his men unobtrusively filtered into the north tree line.

I hadn't been made aware a stay-behind patrol was going to be assigned to ambush the LZ. In the short time we had, I briefed the sergeant as best I could on my suspicions about the VC being out there, and told him to be careful. I felt all along that the enemy were in those north woods; that's one reason I kept up the machine gun, harassing fire. If I had known of the LLRP, I would have put an artillery prep in there before they arrived.

Unfortunately, my premonition was correct. Just thirty minutes later, as I was reporting to Major Bullock at our headquarters at Camp Radcliff, a radio call came in that the LLRP had been ambushed. Three men were dead and a reaction company was on the way to rescue the other two, one of whom was the sergeant; both were wounded.

The enemy had found a lucrative target. We didn't get a single tiger.

Chapter 26

The Degradation Of Ahn

An early First Cavalry Division operations report described the town of An Khe as a "small hamlet in southwest Binh Dinh Province". "Small" may well have been an apt description when the first of the sky troopers arrived, but when the 5/7 Cav got there, the town was sizable by rural Vietnamese standards. A district headquarters for local self-defense units, An Khe was the sole bit of civilization astride National Highway 19 between the key seaport of Quin Nhon on the South China Sea and the major city of Pleiku in the western Central Highlands.

The murky Song Ba (The River Ba) marked the limits of An Khe on the east. The division's giant main base, Camp Radcliff, occupied all the area approximately five hundred meters north of the road, from the Song Ba to a point beyond the western limits of the town. Sandwiched between the base and the highway itself was the old French airfield, two schools and a number of individual homes.

Entering the town from the west, one passed a surprisingly large Catholic church staffed by an old, French speaking, Vietnamese priest. Clustered in the vicinity of the church was a section of larger, more substantial residences than those seen at the other end of town. These were, I

"Shine boys" and juvenile pimps on the streets of An Khe; boy in bowler hat gives the proceeds of his begging to older tough.

Shine boy in An Khe surreptitiously gives author the finger for refusing to have his boots shined

guessed, the possessions of the most prosperous upper crust.

Located between the church on the west and the river on the east was the commercial area, a hodgepodge of shops in open-front buildings, strung in a nearly unbroken wall along both sides of the road which was perhaps forty meters wide. Interspersed here and there among the more substantially built shops were ramshackle, hastily built structures made primarily of corrugated tin. Displayed on the shops which were geared toward selling something to the GIs were brightly painted signs advertising, in English, what the shop sold. "Hong Kong Ladies and Gents Custom Tailoring", "Tam's Laundry Tailor Embroidering" are the two I recall most clearly.

The shops that catered only to the local folks did not have signs. Everyone knew where they were and what they sold. One or two of them served as the local grocery stores which sold spices, salt and other foodstuffs that the locals were unable to grow or manufacture themselves.

Always present were what seemed to be innumerable shoeshine boys, youthful hucksters and street urchins. They didn't annoy an officer once they were told you didn't want a shine, but I knew enlisted men who had their boots polished three or four times in a single day, with a different boy shining each shoe, in an attempt to get rid of them. If they weren't shine boys, they'd be hawking some kind of merchandise such as watches, cigarette lighters, pocket knives, and the like. The urchins who had nothing to sell or no service to render would simply beg.

"You give me p, Joe," was their universal request. By "p" they meant a Vietnamese Piaster, the coin of the realm.

The lowest of them would be trying to interest you in their sister, or someone they called their sister. "You get numba one good time, Joe."

They were a persistent bunch and didn't like taking no for an answer. Once a shine boy accosted me as I was about to take a picture. I shooed him off, only after being required to use a Vietnamese oath. As he walked away, I accidentally caught him in the picture I took. Only after I returned home did I notice that the picture captured his left hand, down at his side, in a surreptitious but unmistakable act of giving me the finger.

Most of these kids looked as if they belonged to someone and were not what the Vietnamese called bui doi—orphans and castaways who lived by their wits on the streets—the "dust of life". These kids looked too clean and well cared for to be bui doi. At least I very much hoped that was the case.

Visiting An Khe by the troops stationed at Camp Radcliff was never encouraged and at times absolutely forbidden. Those going into the town did so on what might be termed semiofficial business. That business was laundry. The men who generally inhabited the rear areas of the division, who didn't expect to wade in muddy rice paddies, and whose uniforms would never be torn trying to get through thorns and brush, attempted to dress as they would if they were back in the States. The Division had a laundry platoon to which one could send soiled clothing and have it cleaned—cleaned, not pressed, certainly not starched, and occasionally not returned at all.

In contrast, the Viets didn't misplace your laundry. They washed, starched and pressed your clothes stiff as a board, then applied a cheap perfume to disguise the smell of the charcoal used to heat the wash water and the pressing irons. Therefore, on any given day, dozens of jeeps and trucks loaded with green, GI laundry bags could be seen in front of An Khe's numerous laundries. Interestingly enough, each of these laundry sorties required the services of three or four men, ostensibly to accomplish the job of loading and unloading. Accordingly, numbers of supply sergeants and warrant officers could be seen lounging in front of their favorite establishment, having a beer on the owner. Meanwhile, the loaders and unloaders roamed the town because, in fact, the laundry owners themselves employed teen-age girls to unload the dirty wash and load the finished product.

Most men at the Cav Main Base had their duties to

perform and they didn't punch in at nine and out at five. As a rule they put in very long hours from early morning to well into darkness, seven days a week, repairing weapons and aircraft, sorting and delivering mail, preparing food, interpreting intelligence information, and a thousand other tasks. They didn't have much time for An Khe, at least at first. However, after the base camp was fairly well established and the Division settled down into a kind of routine, commanders realized that all work and no play isn't the best thing for virile, active young men. Wisdom prevailed and a tightly controlled number of men were permitted to visit the town each day, in addition to the ever present laundry haulers.

Ahn's was one of the better laundries in An Khe. The owner, Mr. Ahn, was a middle-aged Vietnamese with a crew cut graying at the temples, who stayed in the back of the shop. He smiled constantly, said little and worked hard supervising a dozen or more mamma sans who labored amid tubs of steaming wash water and hot irons in the rear of the establishment. Mrs. Ahn was the personality who ran the out-front operation, meeting and greeting the incoming sergeants with their laundry. She would press bottles of cold beer into their hands, bidding them sit in lounge chairs while the sacks of clothes were unloaded by three or four young girls who, after the unloading, sat at the sergeants' feet and smiled nicely. Since no one seemed to know her first name, she was just called Ahn or, more usually, Ann. We assumed she was the owner's wife, although she may have been his sister or anyone else. She was diminutive, less than five feet tall, with her hair cut western style. Ahn always wore the traditional, long, black pajama pants with a colorful blouse worn out at the waist. She was never without a smile. Her English was passable enough to allow her to keep the troops entertained with a constant banter about their comfort and their progress consuming the beer.

Ahn's was the laundry used by the rear echelon of the 5/7 Cav. I wasn't aware of that until one day I decided to break the boredom of the paperwork routine and ride into town with SP/4 Orvin Ravnaas. Rav was one of those rare men who could be trusted to do any job quickly, efficiently and with good cheer. He was a favorite of the Sergeant Major, had been especially chosen to be the battalion commander's driver, and I counted myself fortunate to have had him assigned to me. That day the supply folks asked if he could deliver the laundry. That visit marked the first time I saw Ahn.

Ravnaas exited the jeep and immediately struck up a conversation with Ahn, as the young girls commenced unloading the bags of soiled garments. Orvin was offered a beer and one of the three lounge chairs available. I remained in the jeep, protocol demanding I separate myself from the business of the laundry. I was observing the activity and shooing away shine boys when, from the corner of my eye, I noticed Ahn emerge from the back of the shop with two beers in hand. She gave one to Orvin,

SP/4 Orvin Ravnaas (front) and Ahn, in
front of laundry bags at "Ahn's"

accompanied by a continuing chatter. He sat and she turned to me with the beer in hand, took a single hesitant step and stopped. Ostensibly, my attention was elsewhere—head slightly turned away, eyes shielded by dark glasses—and she would have had to make the overture to get my attention. I imagined her mind at work. This officer seemed to have made himself superior to the mundane around him. To offer him the beer would lower her in his mind, make her much like a common bar girl, a prostitute soliciting business. She was better than that. She was a successful business woman. She would not lower herself. Was it hate, dislike or simple frustration which showed in her face? I wasn't certain. Ahn returned to the back of the shop and reemerged sans beer. I was left without a word from her and allowed to sit in the sunny jeep with no offer of refreshment. Each time I went on a laundry run, her actions were similar.

Economic life was good for the businesses of An Khe. Ahn's shop was piled floor to ceiling with green laundry bags. To keep up with the demand, Mr. Ahn had apparently invested in a dozen or more very large tubs, irons and ironing boards. To heat the water and the irons, he had hundreds of pounds of charcoal stacked in huge bags. There were containers of soap and starch, as well as mounds of craft paper with which to wrap the finished product. Clearly, this was big business for the Ahns. I suspected a big debt also.

Unfortunately, the economic realities of An Khe's business establishments were not factored in when the decision was made by Division to place the town off-limits, except for a very few laundry runs per unit, per week. Word was that the chief of staff hit the roof when he realized how many men were wandering the town during the day, when they were supposed to be working at winning the war. Not only was the town placed off-limits, but, much more critically for the Vietnamese, each unit was told to get as many men as possible up front and out of the rear area. As a result, not only were the numbers of laundry runs greatly reduced, but the number of green bags filled with dirty duds shrank dramatically.

I didn't realize the impact of this policy change until some weeks after that order went into effect. I hitched a ride with the supply sergeant to pick up some laundry, and was surprised to see that An Khe was nearly a ghost town. Some of the shops were already closed, but the impact was most evident to me at Ahn's. She met us as usual, with a large smile, but instead of her normal blouse, she had on a see-through number which clearly exposed her breasts. Additionally, she didn't have a beer in hand, but used that hand to grab the sergeant between his legs while asking him if he wanted a good time. Obviously, she wasn't skilled at grabbing men in that most sensitive spot and hit much too hard, causing the sergeant to hop back quickly in pain. Ahn was not stupid and recognized immediately she'd botched the job, and that the man was not interested in cavorting with any lovelies she might have in the shop's recesses. She started to discuss the laundry with him.

I saw the usual assemblage of pretty girls, none of them more than fourteen years old I guessed, standing off to one side watching Ahn. They had unloaded the very few bags of laundry. Their faces were no longer bright and laughing, but were tinged with fear, and their body language conveyed a desire to quietly scamper away. Their positioning and demeanor were so out of the ordinary that for just an instant I thought they were lined up there as if standing inspection; I had the impossible thought—I wanted it to be impossible—that they were the objects of the good time that Ahn had offered the sergeant. My eyes had shifted to Ahn's breasts. As she turned her attention my way, she caught me looking at them and there was a reflexive movement to turn away from my inquisitive eyes, an attempt to regain her usual modesty. Her pause, however, was only momentary. Ahn knew she was committed and turned full front, affecting a coquettish manner, offering me, as it were, her entire body.

I know I had a look of questioning disbelief and sympathy, perhaps horror, on my face.

"You wanna buy bea, dai uy?" she asked, "good bea—cold—ice cold."

That was the first time she had ever spoken to me directly. I was sitting in the jeep. She came over to me as she waited for an answer and deliberately brushed one breast against my arm. Her eyes showed a kind of forced playfulness, her smile was stiff and contrived.

"No beer, Ahn. Thanks."

She responded with a look just short of defiant hatred at my refusal and walked off to the rear of the shop where I could glimpse just two women laboring at the laundry. Most of the equipment was piled up, unused. Mr. Ahn was nowhere to be seen. Ahn reappeared with finished packages.

The sergeant came out and piled the packages into the back of the jeep. Because some of the men had been sent forward and hadn't paid him for their uniforms, he was short and asked me if I would help pay Ahn. I had more than I required and handed him what he needed and twenty-five extra.

"That's too much," he said.

"Tell her it's a tip, Sarg. Tell her it's for doing a good job with the laundry. Besides, looks like they need it."

"Sure does," he responded.

I knew that was a mistake the moment I did it.

He gave Ahn the money; I couldn't hear what was said. He walked to the jeep. She was looking directly at me. She was angry.

My look, I know, was one of pity. What were we doing to this women who now found herself just short of prostitution, exposing her breasts, perhaps driven to using her children as sex objects in order to survive, to pay off the business debts they incurred catering to Americans? What must the kids think, even if they were only observers? What must her husband feel?

Ahn had the money grasped tightly in her right hand as we pulled away, and then, with a sound that was half an angry scream, half a frustrated sob, she hurled the money towards us. The paper script fluttered into the gutter and was immediately the object of a brawl by the mob of shine boys who had gathered in front of the shop. I looked back and saw Ahn in the midst of the melee, trying to retrieve the money.

Chapter 27

Collecting More Flags

A maxim from ancient China admonishes a soldier to ". . . put out more flags in order to increase your military splendor". In bygone times, battle flags were the honors bestowed on a warrior by his lord for heroic deeds. In our day, a soldier's flags are the medals pinned on his chest by generals, and the comments he receives on his Officer Efficiency Report. To deny that those flags weren't a fundamental force motivating the actions of some officers in Vietnam is to overlook a less than glorious aspect of our participation in the conflict. At times this quest for glory and promotion had disastrous results.

To a significant number of career officers, the raison d'etre for being in Vietnam was to survive a one year tour, gain a combat command for their military records, and amass as many medals and commendations as possible. Vietnam was just a year, but what you did there would greatly affect the next twenty, if you planned to stay in the military.

Many commentators on the war have been critical of the Army policy restricting a combat command in Vietnam to six months. That guideline forced a man into a staff role after half a year, no matter what. Scant regard was given to the officer's abilities or to his successes in combat. While thousands of lieutenant colonels were in the Infantry branch, at any given time the 1st Cav had less than a dozen infantry battalions to command. If a man was restricted to one of those precious positions for just six months of his one year tour, twice as many men could be given a command. In his book *Soldier*, Anthony B. Herbert called those commanders "ticket punchers", racking up "one more credit for their record," with ". . . little motivation except their career impulses . . ."

We were fortunate in our original battalion commander, LTC Trevor W. Swett, an extraordinary officer, very much respected by his troops. Unfortunately, Colonel Swett contracted a serious tropical ailment and was forced to return to the United States. A subsequent battalion commander is the hard-charger I refer to here.

5/7Cav color guard outside headquarters at Camp Radcliff

I can recall this colonel's operations orders because they were signed "For Garry Owen and Glory". Now, by the time of his arrival, I'd seen enough blood, dead bodies and suffering to understand there was damn little glory in what we were doing. To be more specific, there may have been some glory for the battalion commander, but for the guy getting shot at, forget it. No glory in that at all.

There is a place for that gung-ho stuff, a need to foster an esprit de corps in any military unit. That esprit helped to bind the men together into a cohesive fighting force, and for that end it was good. However, "For Gary Owen and Glory" wasn't an esprit builder for the troops—they never saw a formal operations order. That closing was aimed at the generals, for the purpose of collecting more flags.

In the game of oneupmanship played among commanders, our guy was a master. To my knowledge, the 5/7Cav was the only battalion in The Cav which had a color guard outfitted in General Custer era cavalry uniforms, complete with western hats and blue pants with gold stripes. When I went on R & R in Japan, I was given the mission of purchasing a bugle for the color guard. I wondered if someone was to blow it as we charged into battle. Additionally, the Old Man wanted an officers' club, a item unauthorized at battalion level. A permanent "barracks" was built which became the club. Complete with bar, tables, chairs, refrigerators, the works, it was used just once, when the Colonel came to An Khe from the field to officially open it. After he departed, the facility was closed and never utilized for that purpose again.

A lieutenant colonel covering himself with glory needs some servants to keep him primped and spit shined. Most military people will agree that a battalion commander can better utilize his time if someone is looking after his laundry and boots, and insuring his gear is packed when the headquarters is displacing. Those tasks were usually an unofficial, additional duty of the colonel's jeep driver, which is an authorized slot. Our battalion commander not only had a driver to run errands for him, but pulled another man off the line to be his personal lackey. The man he was given for the job was Tom Miles from Bravo Company. Tom was one of the best troopers in the company; when the call went out for a good man to serve the colonel, John Hitti picked Tom. Not too long after Tom started with the colonel, I bumped into him just before dark. He was hauling a large container of water to the Old Man's tent.

"Hey, Tom, how's it going?" I asked.

His "Alright" was far less than enthusiastic.

"What are you doing with that water?"

"Drawing the colonel's hot bath, Sir," he replied.

"Hot bath?" I said, with emphasis on the "hot".

"You heard it right, Captain," and with a surreptitious glance behind him, he said, "Come with me."

In the gathering dusk he led me quickly to the colonel's quarters. Sitting in the middle of the tent floor was a pink bath tub! That is correct. The tub was oval, galvanized, about eighteen inches deep with a capacity I estimated to be about twenty-five or thirty gallons, and it was painted pink. At that moment the monster was sitting about eight inches off the ground on a series of blocks, and burning beneath it were two portable stoves heating the colonel's toilette.

"He likes a hot bath," Miles said sarcastically, probably remembering all those men in the field who had seen hot water just once or twice in half a year.

As an officer I was embarrassed. Rank hath its privileges, but this was pushing it some. I also was thinking of the men in the field.

"Well," I said, commiserating with him, "maybe it beats getting shot at."

"Yea, but I felt a whole lot better about myself out there, Captain."

Taking troops out of the line didn't bother the colonel in the least. He really overstepped his bounds, in my judgment, when he pulled Lieutenant Ralph Cryer out of Bravo Company to be his aide. Since battalion commanders weren't authorized an aide, I wondered why the Old Man had dipped into Bravo again for another personal servant. "I'm an aide of sorts," Ralph said to me with a curious smile when I asked him, "and his photographer."

"His what!"

"His photographer," he reiterated. "That's what I do mostly. The Old Man was looking for someone handy with a camera. That's how I got the job. He has me taking pictures of everything he does. I shoot as many rolls of film a day as I want, no limit. The film, camera, everything is on him."

Ralph's job was to document the colonel's actions. We felt he was looking for his eagle and general's stars, and Ralph was helping him get there.

"That's terrific," I said sarcastically. "An ordinary battalion commander with his own photographer."

"It's shit, that's what it is," was Ralph's sour reply; and then he added, "but it's safe."

Ralph Cryer was dead wrong about that.

The last time I spoke to Ralph was the day the battalion commander was very seriously wounded. Ralph was flown into the battalion TOC helipad aboard one of the few choppers that had been able to get into and out of the battle area in one piece. Although he had a number of shrapnel wounds, not the least of which was a tiny hole in his breast bone right over his heart, Ralph was walking when he got off the bird and gave me his firsthand account of what transpired.

The trouble began when Charlie Company came under fire. The colonel, Major Bullock and Ralph were at LZ English when first reports of the fight came over the battalion net from Bill Brown. When the Old Man received that news, he yelled for Ralph and the Major to follow him as he jumped into his charlie-charlie. They followed, and Ralph found himself flying into a major fire fight, armed only with a .45 caliber pistol borrowed from Duke Frey and, of course, his camera.

MAJ Victor T. "Tom" Bullock and CPT Bill Brown (with helmet)

Once over the battle area, the Old Man tried to assist Bill Brown. The colonel had a platoon from Delta Company on its way to reinforce Company C and the situation was stabilizing. Bill had received a sortie of ARA gun ships which were hitting targets they could identify, and providing fire to keep the Charlie's heads down as his men maneuvered. The real trouble started sometime after 1704 hours, when the Delta Platoon came under fire as it was inserted into the battle area. The platoon commander was killed instantly. The colonel apparently decided to interject himself personally into the fight on the ground by assuming command of the Delta Platoon, or at least a portion thereof. He ordered his pilot to land; he and Ralph got out. Major Bullock was to stay with the bird. The colonel and Ralph were then in the fight and under sniper fire. Fortunately, the lieutenant had the forethought to grab a spare radio when he exited the chopper.

Speaking from the point of view of a small unit commander, what the colonel did was a nightmare. You really don't want two honchos on the ground at the same time, a situation which causes confusion for the enlisted men and the officers, should conflicting orders be given. If a unit is in trouble with its leadership ineffective or incapacitated, then a senior commander should interject himself personally into the situation. Whether that was the case here is a matter for some debate. Bill Brown was reasonably in control of the fire fight and there were other enlisted leaders available to the Delta Platoon. On the other hand, as soon as the Delta Platoon was hit, Dave McCabe, its radio operator, alone with his dead commander, called for immediate assistance. The colonel's decision was a judgment call he had every right to make. Unfortunately, Bill wasn't entirely certain where the colonel was or what he was doing. For his part, the CO didn't have a good feel for what Bill was doing and little hard experience, in Vietnam, working on the ground with troops and supporting fires. The results were devastating.

Ralph thought it was sometime around 1720 hours when the colonel saw an NVA soldier pop up from a bunker on the far side of a shallow ditch. The colonel let fly a few rounds at the Charlie, who scampered back into his hole. At the colonel's request, Ralph asked Captain Brown, through Bill's RTO, to call off the ARA. Almost immediately thereafter, the colonel, accompanied by Dave McCabe, several riflemen and a medic, led the group across the ditch toward the enemy bunker. The men, realizing he was the battalion commander, and doubtless thinking he knew what he was doing vis-a-vis the obvious danger from the ARA, followed him.

Aerial Rocket Artillery was a weapons system consisting of 2.75 inch rockets suspended from pods attached to helicopter gun ships, and fired electronically from the aircraft's cockpit. Seen and heard from the side or rear, they ignite and rush to their target with a roar and a whoosh, exploding shortly thereafter when they strike a solid object. The colonel, Ralph Cryer and the little group of men with them learned the hard way that you don't hear the ARA fire when you are in front of them. The weapon travels faster than sound. First there is the explosion, and then, too late, you hear the rocket approaching.

No one understands fully why the ARA was not lifted. Since it was the last pass the gun ship made, in all probability the pilot simply did not receive the message in time or understand its immediacy. Of course, neither he, Bill nor his RTO could have comprehended the urgency, not knowing that at that very moment the colonel, in his haste to get to the NVA soldier, was leading a charge into the mouth of hell. One thing is for certain—the battalion commander violated a cardinal rule by not confirming that the ARA was lifted, and not waiting a sufficient period of time to insure his order was carried out. The gun ship didn't get the message soon enough and made another pass. Ralph Cryer remembers only the deafening explosions from out of nowhere, the tremendous concussion and blast effects followed by the roar of the rockets, blood, screaming and death. The rockets detonated among and around the small band of men. Everyone was hit with flying metal.

The colonel was very seriously wounded and in great danger of bleeding to death. With his ears ringing, nearly unable to hear, and to his memory in a surrealistic slow motion, Lieutenant Cryer screamed into the radio for Bill to call off the ARA. He then explained what happened. Bill Brown acknowledged, but Ralph had already moved to the medic, only to find him dead, killed instantly. Ralph relieved him of his first aid supplies with which he stanched the colonel's bleeding and no doubt saved his life. Most of the other men were not as bad, except for Dave McCabe who was badly hit in the torso and legs. As noted, Ralph had taken several small chunks of jagged metal in the chest.

The lieutenant's immediate situation was extremely precarious. If the gun ship came around for another run, everyone would surely be killed by the rockets or the chopper's mini-guns. Ralph Cryer could have withdrawn what was left of his men to relative safety. All of them could walk unaided except for McCabe and the colonel, who were rendered senseless by the explosions. However, that would have meant abandoning the Old Man and Dave, and for Ralph that wasn't an option. In what was an act of desperate heroism, they "circled the wagons", determined to fight until a medevac came.

For his part, the enemy commander now seemed to realize that he had our men in a bind and started to close in for the kill. Ralph and his much battered force formed a tiny, stationary perimeter and kept the advancing NVA at bay, while the rest of the battalion tried to get medical aid to them. That proved very difficult. The Battalion TOC logged in the first medevac call from Bill Brown, and thereby obtained their first knowledge that something was very wrong, at 1732 hours.

"Bold Eagle 6 to War Paint—request medevac—War Paint 6 has apparently been hit by ARA."

First to attempt a rescue was Major Bullock in the charlie-charlie. After locating the besieged group, he directed the command and control ship to land and try to get the Old Man and the wounded out. No dice. The NVA were waiting and the aircraft was subjected to intense ground fire. At 1748 hours the TOC logged the following transmission from the Major:

"War Paint 3 to War Paint—Get another charlie-charlie up—battalion commander is hit—I have crash landed in War Paint Charlie-Charlie—alert the Battalion XO—I'm prepared to take over on the ground until Battalion XO arrives."

Lieutenant Cryer's situation was very grim for nearly an hour, the time necessary to sufficiently suppress the enemy fire to attempt another medevac. At 1830 hours a medevac arrived. By that time Ralph's men, down nearly to their last magazine, had been reinforced by some superb troops from the Second Platoon of Charlie Company, who fought their way in to the beleaguered troops. Ralph refused evacuation on that first chopper until the more seriously wounded were taken out. That ship came in and went out under heavy enemy fire, took a considerable number of hits and crashed. Fortunately, and a tribute to the heroism of the medevac crews, in McCabe's words, "there was another ship right behind it, and on we went to safety." Ralph got out later, but the Old Man, because he was so badly wounded, could not be evacuated until after dark.

I was at the evac hospital when the Old Man was brought in, and so were a crowd of television journalists with their cameras. Try as I might to shake the feeling, I could not help at that moment but feel an anger toward the man. Having then been privy to Ralph Cryer's first hand account of what happened, I simply could not shake the belief that the colonel charged into where he shouldn't have been, with his photographer ready to snap pictures.

The record would never show the colonel did anything wrong. Few would challenge his decision, particularly in light of his severe wounds; questioning his actions may seem particularly insensitive and arrogant. However, to me he was playing the game, caught up in the system. His life threatening wounds followed inexorably his need to use an excellent field officer for his own photographer; his need to pull good men off the line to draw a hot bath for him; his need to burden a military unit with the task of hauling around a pink bathtub; his need to sign his orders, "For Garry Owen and Glory", build an unauthorized club, dress his color guard like the cavalry of old; his need for a combat command and medals—for more flags. But to a great degree that was how the promotion system operated. The colonel fell victim to the system; and the TV crews, not Ralph, took his picture.

For certain, however, there was no glory and no pictures of the subordinates in the hospital tents just a few feet away from the wounded hero, and no glory for the troops who fought to their last round of ammunition. There were no pictures of Dave McCabe who lives his life with scars and pain, and no pictures of the dead medic. There were no photographs of Ralph Cryer, who performed his duties as an officer brilliantly that day, saving the colonel's life. The real story wasn't the colonel, but his troops.

Not too many days later, the battalion Executive Officer, who had already relinquished command of the battalion to LTC Andrew Gatsis, came to me with a request.

"Bernie, I want you to write the colonel up for a DSC."

DSC stands for the Distinguished Service Cross, the second highest medal for valor in combat that can be awarded to a soldier. The award ranks just below The Congressional Medal of Honor. I had written a number of citations to that point, many posthumous, for troopers who deserved to receive recognition for actions which were beyond what was expected of them.

I was momentarily shocked at the Major's suggestion and, uncharacteristically dropping the normal tone and demeanor with which I usually responded to a request which is really an order, I challenged him.

"What the hell for, Sir? He didn't do anything but get some guys killed and wounded."

"Grady," he replied, with his jaw tightening. "I want you to write him up for the DSC."

That statement was clearly an order, and my being able to continue arguing with him was testament to the fact that he was an intelligent, fair and good officer.

"Major, how can you compare what the colonel did to what some of our other men have done, and they weren't recognized."

"The Old Man had more to lose. Lieutenant colonels don't have to do as much to get a medal," he replied, turning to leave.

I felt certain the Major didn't really believe the first part of that last statement. Obviously, the dead medic, if he could return, would want to challenge just who had more to lose. He believed every bit of the last part, though.

"Major," I said, "from what Lieutenant Cryer told me of what happened out there, it's going to be tough, but if you want it, you'll have it."

I marveled after he was gone. Obviously, the major wasn't taking it on himself to put in the colonel for the DSC.

That would have had to be already approved by the battalion commander and perhaps Division. But he never said that, never inferred he might not agree with the award recommendation. He was the ideal officer subordinate, a team player, putting out more flags for his commander no matter what, loyal to his perceptions of what was expected to the end. For my part, however, I knew at that moment, finally, absolutely, that I wasn't.

Chapter 28

Someone Else's Daughter

The ditch was located behind the village, between the huts and the scrub brush bordering a stream which fed into the rice paddies. Many villages had drainage ditches of that type, broad and shallow, their purpose being to take the overflow of water off the paddies during the wet season. This one was deeper than most, and at that time of year was muddy, with a few puddles of ugly, greenish water.

The little girl in the ditch resembled a typical Vietnamese teenager, in her early teens was my guess. She had long, black, silky hair drawn back in a pony tail. That hair might have fallen more than halfway down her back had she been standing. At that moment the hair was lying wet and matted beneath her head, with errant strands snaking haphazardly in all directions across the mud. Her complexion was slightly darker than most Vietnamese, but an attractive tan color nonetheless; and her eyes were a beautiful dark brown, although at the time they were glazed with pain or fear or both.

The girl was lying partially on her side and was dressed in a white blouse with an ominous, reddish brown stain on the back. Our medic was kneeling beside her when I arrived. An immensely sensitive and gentle young man, experienced far beyond his years in tending to trauma wounds, he was carefully unbuttoning the blouse, starting from the bottom. She attempted to resist, but could not. Obviously, any movement hurt her, and a grimace crossed her face each time she tried. Her expression, and particularly her eyes, revealed the profound fear any child would experience who was being undressed by a stranger while a group of what she must have thought were ugly giants looked on. Americans are much taller than the average Vietnamese. As she looked up at the five or six men gathered at the scene, we must have seemed ominous—sweat-stained from exertion, a bit wild-eyed and drawn after several hours of battle.

The medic peeled the blouse up toward her shoulders. The fabric had adhered to the skin by congealed blood. The child winced as the blouse came unstuck; a tear or two rolled down one cheek, but she made no sound. One of the men knelt on one knee and stroked her head with his hand, which he had carefully wiped clean on his pant leg. Her eyes opened and she looked up at him. I couldn't see his face, but he must have smiled at her. A very faint smile was returned before she closed her tear-filled eyes again.

On her back was what appeared to be a bullet wound, a long grazing tear ending at a hole, about midway up on the right side. We couldn't tell how serious it was, but the wound looked awful and was oozing blood. The girl seemed to sense we meant her no harm. The medic had been careful not to expose any more of her than necessary. She clutched the blouse tightly with her right hand just below the bust line, apparently intent that it would not be unbuttoned any further. Her eyes were closed and she appeared more relaxed.

Gazing at that frail body, I could discern the subtle beginnings of a woman just above the small hand clutching the blouse. God, what a waste! Someone's little girl, struck down in a war she had no part of, no doubt didn't understand and didn't care about, till now. I wondered to myself if she would ever attain adulthood and what other trauma she would have to endure on the way, but you dared not dwell on those kinds of thoughts—ruined your fighting effectiveness. No, you can't think of the consequences to little girls when you throw thousands of steel jacketed missiles into a village, not when there are people in there shooting back at you. You can't, and the politicians who send you and your enemies there obviously don't comprehend that a bullet has no respect for beauty.

"Who the hell would leave a poor kid alone here like this?"

The question came from one of my troopers who was staring at the sight in disbelief. Based on our experiences since we had landed in Vietnam, he posed a good question. When we made contact with the enemy, our presence was seldom a surprise to them or the villagers in the vicinity. If the Viet Cong or North Vietnamese chose to stand and fight, the villagers would leave beforehand, obviously the smart thing to do. Even if we surprised them, the men of the hamlet would flee, afraid of being mistaken for Viet Cong guerrillas or impressed into the South Viet Army. The women, children and old folks, however, would take cover in the underground bunkers, which were a fixture beside each family hut, and wait out the hostilities. If forced to flee, the women would never abandon the children. The bond between the Vietnamese and their offspring was exceptionally strong. I could say without fear of contradiction that a child would never be abandoned as this one was, no matter what the circumstances, unless the parent was coerced to do so.

"Remember when we got the word the civilians were moving out of the village?" I replied. "The Viet Cong were probably herding them along and mingling with them. The girl had been shot and just couldn't make it. Her mother would have never have left her alone unless she had no choice."

Officially, our mission had been to search and destroy—

search out Charlie and destroy the fellow if we were lucky enough to find him—no sweat. We found him, (more precisely, them), and about a squad of them gave us a rough time. We finally were able to fight our way into the village. More accurately, the enemy pulled off a neat di di out the back door and gave the real estate to us. Just prior to the end of the fight, the colonel, in his command and control chopper, spotted a tightly packed group of women and children leaving the village. The Viet Cong disappeared about the same time; thus my deduction that they probably mixed in with the civilians. They correctly assumed we wouldn't shoot at a bunch of kids and their moms. At some time during the fighting, however, the little girl in the ditch had been shot, and then abandoned when she couldn't leave with the others.

The medic found the girl as we started to consolidate our position and prepared to push forward. I had the feeling that our victory celebration would be short lived. The unmistakable sounds of a battle were filtering through the trees from north of our position. I wanted to be ready to move out if we were ordered to do so.

The only tangible things Charlie Company had to show for our trouble were two wounded of our own and several green rucksacks, typical Army of North Vietnam or Main Force Viet Cong issue. The enemy apparently had abandoned them in order to mix with the civilians. The rucks contained nothing of intelligence value, just personal clothing in the main. One held a battery powered, portable radio. We switched it on, after checking the guts to insure we didn't have a clever booby trap in our hands, and were assaulted with oriental music. The sounds were a discordant, singsong solo by a woman vocalist screeching an off-key tune, accompanied by some sort of string instruments, woodwinds, cymbals and drums.

In that hostile setting, the music evoked a sense of futility. Chinese, French, Japanese and others over the centuries have tried to conquer this land. They are all gone now, replaced by Americans— me and this small band of men I command, who are trying their high-tech hand at quelling the same nationalistic fervor. What gall. What naivete. What futility to believe superior fire power will prevail against a mentality which, in my judgment, subordinates the individual to the cause and looks on time as an ally.

"Kill that miserable racket, will you."

My voice carried an uncharacteristic sharpness which caused the trooper holding the radio to quickly snap it off.

"Jesus," said another, "that shit gives me the creeps for some reason."

The wailing noise died away, replaced by the sounds of the distant battle, now noticeably more pronounced, and the WHOP, WHOP, WHOP of an approaching chopper. I scanned the forested hills rising abruptly to the west and imagined eyes, somewhere up there, watching my every move; I could almost feel a presense waiting for me to make a mistake, plotting my demise, waiting for us to leave this village and their country, knowing that we will eventually, inevitably.

The medic was continuing to work on the girl when my radio man passed me the handset for the battalion net.

"War Paint Six. He's in a hurry."

I checked my watch. We had been in the hamlet less than thirty minutes. I had already ordered second and third platoons to start forward toward the battle sounds. They were to advance about fifty meters and hold. We'd then be positioned to react in the event battalion needed us. At the same time, I didn't want all four platoons bunched up in the confined space of the hamlet in the event the VC decided to give us a few departing 82mm mortar rounds.

I answered the Old Man's call. To that point the battalion net had been clogged with strident transmissions between another of our companies and War Paint Six. The company had run afoul of a large enemy force. They had taken casualties and part of the unit was pinned down. The Old Man needed Charlie Company to pull a flanking maneuver on the Viet Cong and there was no question we needed to get on with the job fast.

I gave the colonel a "Wilco" on his orders, just as a helicopter gunship came overhead and hovered not far above the palm trees shading the village. The chopper hesitated a few seconds and then discharged a prolonged burst from its two mini-guns. The Vietnamese described those weapons as the "Moaning Death". They shoot six thousand rounds per minute and, at that rate of fire, the sound of the individual discharges are indistinguishable, merging together into a deafening, moaning roar. The sound was that of a dentist's drill gone berserk. The noise was so loud that men automatically froze in place, shoulders hunched up involuntarily, as if trying to shut out the nearly overwhelming din.

"Saddle up," I yelled to the men within earshot, as the chopper flew off.

My Executive Officer, John Long, was out in the rice paddies in front of the village, still in the process of trying to get our own wounded flown out. I gave John a squad for security and told him to clean up everything and join us later that evening. Second and third platoon leaders were alerted by radio. The company started to move forward toward the shooting. I had pushed the start button on a machine, so to speak, and it commenced to move.

There will never be a pat formula for decision-making in combat, at least not for the infantry officer, and particularly not for the small unit commander. You simply cannot anticipate or factor-in the noise, the confusion, the unexpected events and the doubts and the fears, all of which influence decisions which must be made in seconds.

That day, amid the deafening mini-guns, incoming sniper fire, sergeants yelling orders, and the general confusion as nearly one hundred men moved forward, my thoughts were focused on the lead platoons where the fighting was most likely to start. In my mind's eye was a picture of a topographic map of the area through which we were moving. I was trying to guess where we might meet the enemy, what I would do if we did, how I would utilize the maneuver element, where the other good guys were, how I could call in my artillery support without hitting my men or them. My mind was awash in the minutiae of the moment, focused on the problem of how to keep my men alive, when another gun ship let fly with mini-guns and aerial rocket artillery. In the middle of that confusion, I heard the medic's voice.

"What about the girl?" he yelled.

"Leave her," I ordered without hesitation, just as the gun ship let fly with yet another prolonged burst.

I really didn't think about that decision; there was no time. John would pick her up as he finished policing up the battlefield. Third Platoon had just made contact with a group of enemy riflemen. The medic went running by me, his aid kits flapping against his sides, trying to catch up with the lead men in order to be closer to where he might be needed.

We drove the enemy before us and relieved the pressure on our sister unit. We accomplished the task without taking any more casualties. Evening found us circling the wagons several thousand meters north of the village where the day started. As I was inspecting the newly forming perimeter, making certain the defensive positions and machine guns were placed properly, a burst of M-16 fire from another part of the perimeter shattered the quiet; this was followed just a short time later by an animal bleating. I soon found the source of the noise. Lying just in front of one platoon position was a water buffalo cow. Standing next to her, leaning against her great bulk, was a very young, pathetic looking buffalo calf, bleating its little heart out. The cow had charged some of my men, apparently attempting to protect the calf which the men didn't realize was nearby. She was killed. The calf, somewhat lighter in color than the cow, with soft black eyes and long, baby fuzz over its back, soon joined the mother; sensing something was very wrong, it started an incessant bleating.

Just before dusk Lieutenant Long flew in with choppers filled with men, food, water and ammunition.

"What's that noise?" he asked, as the chopper sounds faded.

We told him and the others about the buffalo calf which, to that point, had continued bleating for over an hour. The prevailing wisdom held that the noise would stop with the night. As I recall, that notion was advanced by a trooper from Chicago. No one bothered to ask where his water buffalo smarts came from, but we all were hoping he was correct. The sound was getting on everyone's nerves; in addition, the enemy would be able to walk right up to the perimeter with bells on their feet, without anyone hearing them over the unbelievably constant, amazingly loud noise from that little critter. Chicago was wrong. The approaching darkness seemed only to frighten the calf more and the crying continued unabated.

Twilight was always a busy time for company commanders in the field. There were the obligatory tasks to be accomplished—registering defensive artillery concentrations, running communications checks with the platoons and higher ups, checking the perimeter, setting out listening posts, and numerous other responsibilities. The periods just before dark and just before dawn were considered times of particular hazard to infantrymen fighting guerrillas. I'm not certain why. I was never attacked at those times, only in broad daylight. At any rate, there were things to do and precautions to take, and it wasn't until those were accomplished that John and I were able to sit down and discuss the events of the day. Only then did the little girl in the ditch cross my mind.

"What about the girl?" I questioned hopefully.

With a confused look, he asked, "What girl?"

He hadn't found any civilians, no wounded little girl, didn't realize she was there.

There were only a few decisions I made in Vietnam for which I am profoundly sorry. That was one. I'd give a lot to have the opportunity to remake it. There are any number of other courses of action I could have taken at that moment. Many of them ran through my mind as I sat there absorbing the impact of what John told me, filled with thoughts of the girl and what might have befallen her by that time. I must have looked shaken, knowing she might be out there, now in the dark, laying in that stinking ditch, hurting, bleeding perhaps, and all alone. One of the RTOs fathomed what was going through my mind and tried his best to help.

"Don't bother about it, Sir," he said. "It's not your fault, not your problem. She was someone else's kid."

"Someone else's daughter," I mumbled to myself, nearly speechless with the thought that the RTO was already speaking of her in the past tense.

The gathering night had started to turn colder than normal. A heavy, bone chilling mist would set in by dawn. There was little perceptible sound except for the bleating of the buffalo calf every fifteen seconds or so with nearly foghorn regularity, until a burst of fire from an M-60 shattered the stillness and seemed to echo endlessly up the hills to our rear; and then, silence.

Chapter 29

DEROS

On August 5, 1967, Major Bullock and Captains Crocket and Grady arrived at the 1st Cavalry Division Transfer Station to begin our journey home. DEROS had come for us—the Date of Expected Return from Overseas Station—the end of our tour in Vietnam. After processing, we lined up to board a C-130 that would take us to Cam Ranh Bay, thence on to the United States. A band was playing as the men filed on the aircraft which was parked at nearly the exact spot where 1st Sergeant Hare and I unloaded 363 days prior, and thereby mounted the Vietnamese tiger. I turned and looked at the countryside once more. The sky was as pristine blue as it was a year before. Gorgeous, white cumulus clouds towered into the heavens. The land was still verdant. To the eye nothing had changed, but in the heart everything was different.

Somewhere, in the mountains to the west, the 5th Battalion 7th Cavalry was still operating, but all of the 750 magnificent men who first filled its ranks at Fort Carson were no longer on duty. They had given their best to their country as ordered. Almost eighty of those superb soldiers were already home in body bags, including the Top. They were the men who would never dismount the tiger, those who would be imperfectly remembered each Memorial Day thereafter, those whose names would be etched forever on the black granite monument. The number of wounded was difficult to determine, but our best guess was that only about sixty percent of the 750 original troopers were still in-country at the end.

The band ceased for a moment. I took a last deep breath of Vietnam just as the wind blew a foul odor off the nearby paddies. No cigar smell masked the stench.

"You were right, Top," I couldn't help saying to no one in particular. "Smells just like Korea."

Davey Crocket overheard me and asked, "How do you know? You've never been to Korea."

At that moment the aircraft engines came to life with a whistling, whining, popping sound.

"My first sergeant told me," I answered over the din, but he didn't hear.

Inside the bake-oven belly of the plane the air was sultry, oppressive. The engines swirled dust and the exhaust of aviation fuel through the back cargo ramp over our already sweating bodies. A jeep with a post mounted machine gun came into view and disappeared. The band, barely audible, had resumed playing. The rousing, martial music may have been appropriate for replacements just arriving, but for us the piece should have been a requiem.

The aircraft taxied, revved its four turboprops, sped down the runway and lurched toward the heavens. I flew off the back of the tiger.

Epilogue

A Better Way

In early October of 1966, a man whose name I did not know died. He was clad in a North Vietnamese Army uniform and was half-hidden in a spider hole along the side of a rice paddy dike, somewhere in central Vietnam. Having received an obviously terminal wound, he had been abandoned by his comrades who left him to die after they stripped him of nearly everything. He had no weapon, no food or water, no documents or personal papers in his possession save one. Clutched tightly in his hand was a small, black and white snapshot of a Vietnamese woman and a cute little girl perhaps four years of age, both smiling into the camera. The photo was soggy and crumpled. What appeared to be some Vietnamese writing on its reverse was smeared.

Our medic had given the suffering soldier a shot to ease his pain, and only after the narcotic took effect could he pry the picture from the man's grasp. The Doc studied the photo pensively, handed it to me, and walked off to be with himself.

"Must be his family," he said in a choked voice.

"I guess so," I answered.

"The guy's crying, Captain," said First Sergeant Hare. "Looks like he wants that picture back."

The man was reaching upward, apparently for the photo. I knelt and returned it to his hand. There were tears running down his dirt streaked face and indistinct sobs matched a convulsive shaking of his body. At first I thought he was in pain, but his eyes had the glaze of morphine. The tears were not from any physical suffering. As I watched him struggle to glimpse and to focus on the snapshot once more, I understood those tears were shed because he realized that all he had left to him in this world, all that he loved and held dear, were represented by his picture; and he knew quite certainly he would never see them or speak to them or hold them close to him again. The soldier appeared to be struggling against the inevitability of his death and he looked into my eyes with fear and dread etched into his face.

I smiled at him and said quietly, "You can let go," as I touched his well-muscled shoulder, squeezing gently.

He clutched his family to his chest, relaxed visibly and died.

The first sergeant, who fought in World War II and Korea, came to attention and paid his respects to a fellow soldier with a salute. That old warrior who had seen too much—and who himself had only a few more weeks before he would be just a memory in the minds of his wife, son and two daughters—asked the heavens as he walked away, "God, isn't there a better way?"

We seldom had the time or the inclination to bury the enemy in Vietnam, but this man we laid to rest in the spider hole, still clutching his family. I was hard and tough then, as were most of us who fought. An understanding of the terrible waste that is war had not yet registered with me. At that time, perhaps, I didn't want it to. In reality, I didn't dare let it.

As I write, more than twenty-seven years have elapsed, and more conflicts have caused men, women and children to die because we have not yet found a better way. And we must. Not only because those whose names crowd the walls of the black granite monument commemorating their sacrifice are owed nothing less, but, more importantly, because future generations must not be lulled into our same mistakes. They cannot be permitted by some sense of machismo, invincibility, self-righteousness or base ignorance to think war is anything but an atrocity writ large, and they must never stop seeking a better way than armed conflict to resolve disputes among peoples and nations.

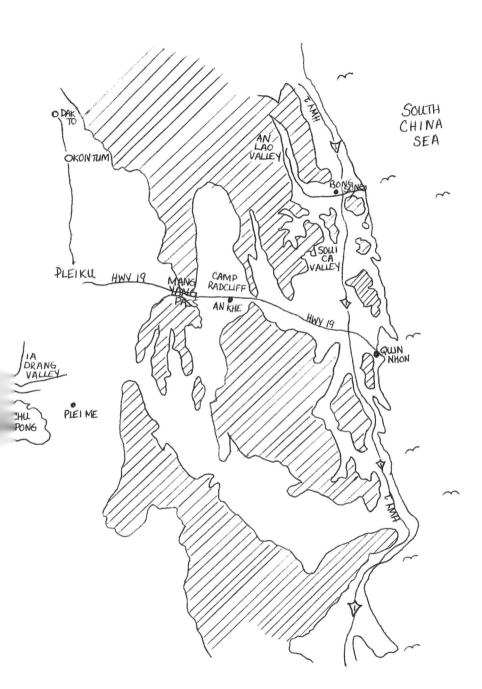

South Vietnam Central Highlands

CENTRAL-COASTAL AND NORTHEASTERN BINH DINH PROVINCE

ORGANIZATIONAL CHART
5TH BATTALION (AIRMOBILE) 7TH CAVALRY*
Assignments when deployed, August 1966

Battalion Commander-LTC Trevor W. Swett Jr.
Executive Officer-MAJ Robert Jennings
Sergeant Major-CSM Robert Meyers

Support Functions
Adjutant (S-1) Personnel Officer-CPT Bill Brown
Intelligence (S-2)-CPT Walt Swain
Operations (S-3)-MAJ Victor T. "Tom" Bullock
   S-3 Air-CPT Martin C. "Duke" Frey
Supply (S-4)-CPT Davey Crocket
   WO1-Oscar Igoe
Battalion Surgeon
Chaplain-MAJ Tom Widdel
Headquarters Company-CPT Jerry Houston, CO

Infantry Companies
Company A (Alpha)-CPT A.J. Wise, CO

Company B (Bravo)-CPT John Hitti, CO
   1LT Bernard Grady, XO
   2LT Bill Bronson, 1ST PLT
   2LT Bill Kail, 2ND PLT
   2LT Jon Merton, 3RD PLT
   2LT Ralph Cryer, MORTARS
   1ST SGT Dayton L. Hare

Company C (Charlie)-CPT Larry Budge, CO
   1LT John Long, XO
   2LT Rick Belt, 1ST PLT
   2LT Doug McCrary, 2ND PLT
   2LT Dave Lytle, 3RD PLT
   1ST SGT Haskell Westmoreland

Company D (Delta)

Selected individuals and subunits mentioned in text

Glossary

AK-47:   Kalashnikov Assault Rifle. Soviet made assault rifle, semiautomatic or automatic, 7.62mm.

ARA: Aerial Rocket Artillery. 2.75 inch rockets fired from pods mounted on HU-1B, Huey helicopters. Highly effective close fire support weapon for the infantry.

Artillery Prep: Concentrated artillery fire placed on a landing zone just prior to the arrival of the infantry in helicopters.

ARVN: Army of the Republic of South Vietnam. A soldier or unit belonging to the South Vietnamese Army.

Battalion: The primary infantry tactical maneuvering unit for the 1st Cavalry Division. Consisted initially of a headquarters company, three rifle companies (A, B, & C), and a heavy weapons company (D). The heavy weapons company consisted of mobile recoilless rifles and heavy mortars (4.2 inch). Because this configuration was inconsistent with the airmobile concept and jungle fighting, Delta Company was changed to a fourth infantry company. A battalion numbered approximately 750 men.

Battery: A basic, tactical artillery unit corresponding to an infantry company. The 5/7Cav was supported mainly by the 1/21 Artillery (105mm), called the "Big Voice of Garry Owen"; the 1/30 Artillery (155mm); and, occasionally, by self propelled 8 inch guns.

Bird: Any of the several types of helicopters organic to the 1st Cavalry Division.

Brigade: Next higher command above a battalion.

C-4: Very powerful plastic explosive carried in one pound blocks; is the explosive charge inside a claymore mine.

C-130: Large cargo or troop carrying aircraft capable of trans ocean flights. The C-130 was the workhorse aircraft in Vietnam with its relatively short take-off and landing characteristics.

Call Sign: The radio code name, known only to American forces, which identified a particular unit. "War Paint" was the original call sign for the 5/7 Cav. War Paint 6 was the battalion commander, War Paint 5 was the battalion executive officer, War Paint 4—the S-4, War Paint 3—the S-3, and so on. Similarly, Comanche Brave 6 was John HItti's original call sign when he commanded Company B; as XO, mine was Comanche Brave 5. As commander of Company C, my call sign was Bold Eagle 6, Eagle 5 was the XO, Eagle Four-Six the fourth platoon leader, and so on. Bold Eagle 7 was the company first sergeant.

Charlie-Charlie: The command and control helicopter found at battalion level and higher. Also known as a C&C, this chopper carried a bank of radios capable of coordinating simultaneously with the line rifle companies, brigade, division, and with tactical support aircraft. 5/7Cav commander used his charlie-charlie to maintain personal contact with his four, widely dispersed companies in the field.

Charlie or
Victor Charlie: The Viet Cong.

CH-47:   The Chinook cargo helicopter; workhorse of the 1st Cavalry Division. Dual rotor blades on this chopper made it possible to carry a full platoon of troops or tons of cargo. This helicopter was the prime mover for the organic division artillery. It simply used a sling suspended from its underbelly to transport artillery pieces.

Claymore: The Claymore Antipersonnel Mine. A crescent shaped, antipersonnel mine slightly larger than the typical paperback novel, packed with one pound of C-4 explosive behind 600 small steel balls. The mine was detonated by a blasting cap fired from a distance by a small, hand held, electrical generating device.

CO: Commanding Officer.

Company: Primary maneuver unit of a battalion. Commanded by a captain with an Executive Officer as second in command and a 1st Sergeant as senior NCO. Consisting of approximately 175 men in the field at full strength, comprised of three rifle platoons and a mortar platoon.

CP: Command Post.

CPT: Captain.

C's: C-rations. Canned combat rations which came as a single meal. A meal consisted of a 10 oz. main portion (e.g. Meatballs and Beans in Tomato Sauce), a can of three crackers, a can of jelly or cheese to cover the crackers, a 4 oz. can of desert such as fruit cocktail, two pieces of chewing gum, and a packet of toilet paper.

Command Net: Radio frequency assigned to a unit's tactical units over which unit commanders could communicate.

Dai Uy: Vietnamese words for captain, pronounced "die we".

DT's or Delta Tangos: Defensive targets. Preregistered, artillery targets around a defensive perimeter called into the support artillery battery usually prior to dark. The forward artillery observer or company commander could adjust the battery from the DT's to hit enemy targets.

EM: Enlisted man, as distinguished from a warrant officer or an officer.

Enfilade: Shoot along the long axis of an enemy force or position.

F-4: Air Force, close tactical support, jet fighter aircraft.

FAC: Forward Air Controller. Air Force officer flying a Bird Dog who adjusts artillery fire or air strikes from jet fighters.

Firebase: An artillery firing position. A landing zone where an artillery unit is set up to provide fire support to line companies maneuvering against the enemy.

Field of Fire: A clear area where a weapon can effectively engage the enemy.

Fire team: Primary maneuver unit of a squad. (See Squad)

FO: Forward Observer. Specifically, an artillery forward observer whose job it was to lay and adjust artillery fire. One FO, usually a lieutenant, was assigned to each company.

Garry Owen: Motto of the United States Seventh Cavalry since the time of General George Armstrong Custer.

Graves Registration (GR):   Unit responsible for processing the dead.

Gunship: Heavily armed, HU-1B helicopter from the 2/20 Artillery used for close fire support. Gunships were variously equipped with ARA, mini-guns, 40mm cannons, or heavier munitions.

H & I: Harassing and interdicting fire. This is a preplanned concentration of random fire against suspected enemy targets or simply at random in free-fire zones to harass the enemy and deny him free movement.

HHC: Headquarters and Headquarters Company. The fifth company in the battalion to which all staff personnel were assigned.

High Angle Fire: Explosive rounds fired by artillery or mortars which travel in a high arc, as opposed to direct fire weapons such as a rifle or machine gun.

HQ: Headquarters, at any command level.

Huey: Primary, utility helicopter used by the 1st Cav for troop movement and assault, as medevac choppers, and as command and control birds.

KIA: Killed in action.

Klick: Slang term for a kilometer, 1000 meters.

LAW: Light Antitank Weapon. A shoulder fired, 66mm rocket, antitank weapon shot from a collapsible firing tube which was discarded after use.

Log Bird: Name for a resupply helicopter, "Log" coming from the word logistics.

LP: Listening Post. A patrol of men, usually two or three, placed in a fixed position forward of a defensive perimeter whose duty it was to listen for and warn of approaching enemy units and then retreat into the perimeter.

LT: Lieutenant.

LTC: Lieutenant colonel.

LZ: Landing Zone for helicopters or any semi-permanent facility.

M-14:   Principal, American, shoulder fired, infantry rifle prior to the introduction of the M-16.

M-16:   Principal, American, shoulder fired weapon used in Vietnam. Automatic or semiautomatic rifle with a 20 round magazine. Very light weight weapon (7.6 pounds), much of which was made of plastic. When properly maintained, a very dependable weapon firing a 5.56mm round at very high velocity, producing considerable damage when it strikes a target.

M-60: Principal, American light machine gun used in Vietnam. Gas operated, belt fed weapon firing a 7.62mm round. Very dependable and effective weapon when properly maintained. Two M-60's were authorized per rifle platoon.

M-79: American, single shot, shoulder fired weapon which launched a 40mm grenade. Highly accurate, very effective weapon which replaced the rifle grenade. Two grenadiers were authorized per rifle squad.

Mask: Anything that interferes with the trajectory of a weapon. If friendly troops get in a gun's line of fire the weapon is said to be masked and cannot fire.

Medevac: Evacuation of wounded by helicopter.

MIA: Missing in Action. This term was not only used for men who were unaccounted for in action but also for the dead, prior to being declared KIA, who had not as yet been positively identified.

Mini-gun: An electrically operated, machine gun mounted on gun ships, capable of firing 6000 rounds per minute of 7.62 ammunition.

MOS: Military Occupational Specialty

MPC: Military Payment Certificates.

NCO: Noncommissioned officer. An enlisted man holding the rank of Sergeant E-5 (SGT), Staff Sergeant E-6 (SSG), Sergeant First Class E-7 (SFC), Master Sergeant E-8 (MSG), First Sergeant E-8 (1st SGT), Sergeant Major E-9.

NVA: North Vietnamese Army. This was the regular, North Vietnamese Army soldier as opposed to the guerrilla or VC.

Officer: Rank in the military higher that a warrant officer (WO) and an enlisted man (EM). 2d Lieutenant O-1 (2LT), 1st Lieutenant O-2 (1LT), Captain O-3 (CPT), Major O-4 (MAJ), Lieutenant Colonel O-5 (LTC), Colonel O-6 (COL), General Officer.

Platoon: Primary maneuver unit of a company. Commanded by a Lieutenant with a Sergeant First Class as second in command and senior NCO. Approximately 47 men at full strength, divided into four squads.

Point Man or Point: Lead man or lead unit in an infantry movement.

PRC-25: Principal infantry radio used in Vietnam called a Prick Twenty-Five.

Punji Stick: A sharpened, fire hardened, bamboo stick which is shaved very sharp and placed in the ground as a barrier to impede progress or as a passive weapon to inflict wounds.

R&R: Rest and relaxation leave. Each man stationed in Vietnam for one year was afforded one week of leave in Tokyo, Hong Kong, or other cities in Southeast Asia or Hawaii. Additionally, enlisted men were afforded one additional three day leave in Vung Tau or Cam Ranh Bay.

RTO: Radio Telephone Operator. The man who carried the PRC-25 or operated any kind of radio or telephone equipment.

RF-PF's or
Ruff-Puffs: South Vietnamese Regional Force-Popular
                         Force soldiers. Locally recruited, military
                         forces employed within their home districts
                         to guard strategic hamlets, bridges, strong
                         points, and the like.

RVN: Republic of South Vietnam. South Vietnam.

S-1:   The "Adjutant"—staff officer responsible for
                         personnel matters. At battalion level, usu-
                         ally a captain. Smallest unit assigned formal
                         staff officers is battalion.

S-2:   The Intelligence Officer—staff officer re-
                         sponsible for enemy intelligence estimates.
                         Usually a captain.

S-3:   The Operations Officer—staff officer re-
                         sponsible for planning all combat operations.
                         Usually a major.

S-3/Air: Staff officer responsible for tactical air sup-
                         port (Air Force or Navy) and division heli-
                         copters. Works for S-3, usually a captain.

S-4:   Supply Officer—staff officer responsible for
                         logistical support. Usually a captain.

Sit rep: A radio report of the tactical situation as it
                         exists at the time of transmission.

SKS: A Russian, 7.62mm, semiautomatic rifle
                         somewhat similar to the M-14.

Slick: A huey helicopter.

SOP: Standard Operating Procedure. Formal writ-
                         ten doctrine concerning the correct way to
                         accomplish any task.

Squad: Primary tactical unit of a platoon. Commanded by a Staff Sergeant. Comprised of eleven men divided into two five man fire teams.

TOC: Tactical Operations Center. The battalion headquarters and operations area where all communications were monitored. From this location the Battalion or S-3 controlled all battalion operations in the field. Called the "Tock".

VC: Viet Cong.

Volley: The simultaneous discharge of more than one weapon. An artillery volley would be the firing of a single round from each of the three guns in the battery.

WIA: Wounded in Action.

Warrant Officer: A staff officer, usually in a special skill assignment such as pilot, ranking just above an enlisted sergeant and just below an officer.

XO: Executive Officer. Second in command of a company, battalion, or brigade.

81: Short for an 81 millimeter mortar. The primary, indirect fire weapon carried by the airmobile infantry rifle company. The 81mm mortar had the capability of firing a variety of ordinance, a high explosive round for concussion and destructive effects, a white phosphorus round for burning and producing smoke, a flare round for illumination at night, and a smoke round for marking targets.

105: Short for the 105mm howitzer.

155: Short for the 155mm howitzer.

Order Form

Please send

_____ copies *On the Tiger's Back* @$12.95 _____

Tax, Maine sales only, add 6% ($.77) _____

Shipping $2.25 first book,
$1.00 ea. additional book.
Priority shipping, $4.00 first book _____

TOTAL _____

Send check or money order to
Biddle Publishing Co.
PO Box 1305 #103   207-833-5016
Brunswick, Maine 04011

Name _____

Address _____

_____

Phone _____